AN ESSAY ON GRAMMAR-PARSER RELATIONS

Publications in Language Sciences

Publications in Language Sciences is a series of monographs in theoretical linguistics and its more formal satellite fields of scientific inquiry. It is intended to provide an opportunity for scholars working within these areas to report rapidly on research either terminated or in some definite stage of progress. Ideally, in these publications interest, inspiration, and openmindedness go hand in hand.

Ger J. de Haan
Leo Wetzels
Wim Zonneveld
editors

Other books still available in this series:

1. W. Zonneveld and F. Weerman
   Linguistics in the Netherlands 1977-1979
2. G. de Haan
   Conditions on Rules
4. P. Kiparsky
   Explanation in Phonology
5. A.J. Vitale
   Swahili Syntax
6. R.M. Martin
   Logico-Linguistic Papers
7. S. Dik
   Functional Grammar
9. S. Strauss
   Lexicalist Phonology of English and German
12. H. Bennis and W.U.S. van Lessen Kloeke
    Linguistics in the Netherlands 1983
13. M.P.R. van den Broecke, V.J. van Heuven and W. Zonneveld
    Sound Structures
15. Mieke Trommelen
    The Syllable in Dutch
16. Carlos Gussenhoven
    On the Grammar and Semantics of Sentence Accents
18. Jaap van Marle
    On the Paradigmatic Dimension of Morphological Creativity
19. Larry M. Hyman
    A Theory of Phonological Weight
20. Frits Stuurman
    Phrase Structure Theory in Generative Grammar
21. H. Haider and M. Prinzhorn
    Verb-Second Phenomena in Germanic Languages
23. Leo Wetzels and Engin Sezer (eds.)
    Studies in Compensatory Lengthening
24. Osvaldo Jaeggli and Carmen Silva-Corvalán (eds.)
    Studies in Romance Linguistics
25. Carol Neidle and Rafael A. Nuñez Cedeno (eds.)
    Studies in Romance Languages
26. John Anderson and Jacques Durand (eds.)
    Explorations in Dependency Phonology
27. Frans van Coetsem
    Loan Phonology and the Two Transfer Types in Language Contact
28. David Birdsong and Jean-Pierre Montreuil (eds.)
    Advances in Romance Linguistics
29. M. Everaert, A. Evers, R. Huybregts and M. Trommelen (eds.)
    Morphology and Modularity
30. W. de Haas
    A Formal Theory of Vowel Coalescence
31. F. Weerman
    The V2 Conspiracy
32. Wendy Sandler
    Phonological Representation of the Sign
33. P.Th. van Reenen and M.E.H. Schouten
    New Methods in Dialectology
34. Ellis Visch
    A Metrical Theory of Rhythmic Stress Phenomena
35. Jean-Pierre Angoujard
    Metrical Structure of Arabic

J. van de Koot

AN ESSAY ON GRAMMAR-PARSER RELATIONS

1990
FORIS PUBLICATIONS
Dordrecht - Holland/Providence RI - U.S.A.

Published by:
Foris Publications Holland
P.O. Box 509
3300 AM Dordrecht, The Netherlands

Distributor for the U.S.A. and Canada:
Foris Publications USA, Inc.
P.O. Box 5904
Providence RI 02903
U.S.A.

CIP-DATA

Koot, J. van de

An Essay on Grammar-Parser Relations / J. van de Koot. - Dordrecht [etc.] : Foris. -
(Publications in Language Sciences ; 36)
Ook verschenen als proefschrift Utrecht, 1990. - Met lit. opg.
ISBN 90 6765 497 3
SISO 805.1 UDC 801.5
Trefw.: grammatica.

ISSN 0924-6568
ISBN 90 6765 497 3

Printed in The Netherlands by ICG Printing, Dordrecht.

". . .trying to understand perception by studying only neurons is like trying to understand bird flight by studying only feathers. . ."
(Marr 1982:p.27)

Table of Contents

Acknowledgements xi

Preface 1

Chapter 1: The Relation Grammar-Parser 5
- 1.1 Introduction 5
- 1.2 The legitimacy of the competence-performance distinction 6
  - 1.2.1 The mentalistic approach 6
  - 1.2.2 Marr (1982) 7
- 1.3 The competence-performance distinction and the concept of psychological reality 14
  - 1.3.1 The common enterprise 14
  - 1.3.2 Grammar-parser correspondences 16
    - 1.3.2.1 I/O Correspondence 16
    - 1.3.2.2 Degenerate I/O Correspondence 19
    - 1.3.2.3 Strong Equivalence 21
    - 1.3.2.4 Covering Equivalence 22
    - 1.3.2.5 Metastrong Equivalence 22
    - 1.3.2.6 Overview 23
- 1.4 A historical survey 24
  - 1.4.1 The Derivational Theory of Complexity 24
  - 1.4.2 Lexical Functional Grammar 26
  - 1.4.3 Generalized Phrase Structure Grammar 28
  - 1.4.4 Performance grammars 30
  - 1.4.5 Parsifal (Marcus 1980) 32
- 1.5 The relation grammar-parser and so-called functional explanations 33
  - 1.5.1 Fodor's (1985) classification of functional explanations 33
  - 1.5.2 Explanations of properties of the competence level at the algorithmic level: efficiency and strategy 35
  - 1.5.3 Explanations of properties of the competence and algorithmic levels at the hardware level 37
- 1.6 Conclusion 37

Chapter 2: Explaining Subjacency: An Overview 39
- 2.1 Introduction 39
- 2.2 The Marcus parser 40
  - 2.2.1 The Determinism Hypothesis 40
  - 2.2.2 The data structures 42
  - 2.2.3 The process structure 45
    - 2.2.3.1 Pattern-action rules 46
    - 2.2.3.2 The primitive actions 47
    - 2.2.3.3 Three types of rules 48
  - 2.2.4 An example parse 50
- 2.3 Some apparent counterexamples to lookahead 54

2.3.1 Parsing with assertion sets 55
2.3.2 Some constructions claimed to be incompatible with lookahead 59
2.3.2.1 Lookahead and the structure of NPs 59
2.3.2.2 Frazier and Rayner's (1982) reading experiment 61
2.3.2.3 Short garden paths 64
2.4 Some suggestions for a theory of the buffer 66
2.5 Berwick and Weinberg's modified Marcus parser 67
2.6 Formal properties of the Marcus parser: LR(k), BCP(m,n), and LRRL(k) grammars 69
2.7 LRRL(k) parsing and functional explanation 73
2.7.1 Berwick and Weinberg's functional explanation of Subjacency 73
2.7.2 A critical examination: LRRL(k) parsing and restricted annotation 75
2.7.3 Why GPSG combined with LRRL(k) parser explains Subjacency as well 78
2.7.4 Summary of results 80
2.8 Van de Koot (1987): barriers and determinism 80
2.8.1 Some basic properties of the Barriers framework 81
2.8.2 A review of the island violations 88
2.8.3 L-marking as a constraint on immediate attachment 90
2.8.4 Criticism 95
2.9 Summary 96

Chapter 3: Grammatical Constraints and Determinism 97

3.1 Preview 97
3.2 LRRL(k) parsing and locality in chains 99
3.2.1 The analysis of wh-movement 99
3.2.2 Traces versus features: antecedent government 99
3.2.3 Towards a generalized condition on chain links: wh-islands 102
3.2.4 Adjunction and grammar size 107
3.3 Deterministic chain formation 108
3.3.1 Introduction 108
3.3.2 Adjunct attachment as a last resort strategy 108
3.3.3 Licensing the creation of covert categories in A'-position 113
3.3.4 The form and interpretation of adjunct-operator chains 117
3.3.5 Why the insertion of empty operators must be antecedent-dependent 118
3.3.6 Extraction from adjuncts and adjunct parasitic gaps 120
3.3.7 Extraction from subjects and subject parasitic gaps 122
3.3.8 Extraction from objects and the non-existence of object parasitic gaps 123
3.3.9 Licensing the creation of traces in A-positions 124
3.3.10 Why parasitic gaps cannot be licensed by a wh-trace in subject position 129
3.4 Summary of results 131

Chapter 4: Epilogue 133

4.1 Summary 133
4.2 Conclusions: The Relation Grammar-Parser Revisited 135

Bibliography 141

Index 147

Samenvatting 153

Curriculum Vitae 157

Acknowledgements

It is with great pleasure that I thank the following people who have all in one way or another contributed to the preparation of this dissertation.

I wish to express my sincere gratitude to my supervisors Ger de Haan and Louis des Tombe for their stimulating support throughout the project. A special word of thanks to Ger for his respectful patience and quiet encouragement in both linguistic and non-linguistic matters.

I am grateful to Arnold Evers, Michael Moortgat, Henk Verkuyl, Fred Weerman and Frans Zwarts for their work as the members of my thesis committee. I also thank the members of the committee of supervisors: Riny Huybregts, Steven Krauwer, Jan Landsbergen, David Lightfoot and Frans Zwarts.

I have greatly benefitted from comments made by Peter Coopmans, Jan Don, Arnold Evers, Ger de Haan, Ed Ruys and Louis des Tombe on an earlier draft of this work, as well as from many discussions with them.

Albert Leenders, Martin Everaert, Jan Don and Wim de Haas all at some time in the past shared a room with me and inspired me with many stimulating and very enjoyable discussions. Especially during the last year of my research Ed Ruys became a regular participant in these daily workshops. I feel I owe a lot to their collective wit and enthusiasm.

I would like to thank all my former colleagues at Trans 10 in Utrecht for having made it a better and more cheerful place for me to work (and have lunches). The OTS/linguistics secretariat has always been the ideal place to go for any researcher in a creative impasse: I thank Hellen König, Gerda van Kampen and Marie-Louise de Ridder for nursing me back to creativity on an almost daily basis. A special thank you goes to Ploon Versteeg for a generous supply of quality coffee.

I am grateful to the Foundation of Linguistic Research, financed by the Netherlands Organization for Research (NWO), which supported the research of which this document is the final result (grant 300-163-024). I would particularly like to thank NWO for the financial support I received for my visit to MIT in the fall of 1987. Many people have made my stay in the US a very valuable and stimulating experience. I would like to thank the following people: Noam Chomsky, Marco Haverkort, Mark Johnson, Ray Jackendoff, Mike Kashket, Marta Lujan, James Pustejovsky and Sara Rosen and friends (especially for the sushi-dinner). I also had the opportunity to visit the linguistics department of the University of Maryland. I thank David Lightfoot, Amy Weinberg and Norbert Hornstein for some interesting discussions, and David Lightfoot and Sari

Hornstein for a terrific meal.

I thank Mike Kashket, Steve Abney, Eric Ristad, and Mitch Marcus for several lengthy exchanges via electronic mail.

I am grateful to my present colleagues at the department of phonetics and linguistics of University College London, and in particular to Neil Smith, for their encouragement and for giving me the opportunity to finish this document.

A special thank you goes to Martin Everaert and Simone van Weteringen for giving me a pied-a-terre in Utrecht and much more.

Finally, I would like to thank my parents, my brothers and all my dear friends for their continuous love and support.

Preface

The text that follows is an investigation into the relationship between grammars and parsers. It is conducted at two levels. The first part (chapter 1) is a rather philosophical study of possible grammar-parser relations. The second part (chapters 2 and 3) is an inquiry into the relationship between current versions of transformational grammar and a deterministic model of the human sentence processor, specifically an LRRL(k) parser.

The work as a whole is intended as a contribution to the research paradigm that developed from the work of Marcus (1980). This book marked the beginning of renewed interest in parsing on the part of linguists working in the field of transformational grammar, following a long period of relative inactivity brought about by the failures of a long series of experiments conducted in the sixties and early seventies.

In those early days of the theory of transformational grammar it was hoped that psycholinguistic experiments could provide evidence that transformations were concretely realized in the human sentence processor. When this hypothesis of "direct realization" was tested under the Derivational Theory of Complexity and proved to be untenable, many linguists, psychologists and computationalists turned their backs upon transformational grammar, often in search of theories that would do a better job at laying the foundations for a psycholinguistically plausible model of human sentence processing.

In retrospect, the general disappointment can be traced to a lack of appreciation of the competence-performance distinction and of the range of hypotheses about the grammar-parser relation that it made available. The Derivational Theory of Complexity was exactly what its name says it was: a theory. It was designed to test the hypothesis of "direct realization", which was just one of a large number of possible hypotheses about the way a transformational grammar might be realized in a perceptual model. Therefore, the failure of the Derivational Theory of Complexity refuted the hypothesis of "direct realization" but not the theory of transformational grammar.

Marcus's *A Theory of Syntactic Recognition for Natural Language* takes up the threads where they were lost in the early seventies. This work is first of all an attempt to provide independent motivation for a particular parsing model and to show that this parser realizes a transformational grammar. In the course of his investigations, Marcus became aware that certain universal conditions on transformational rules proposed by Chomsky and others seemed to follow in a natural way from properties of this independently motivated parser. Following in Marcus's tracks, Berwick (1982) and Berwick & Weinberg (1984) proposed several modifications to the original parsing model and argued that constraints of current transformational grammar conspire with certain properties of this modified parser to explain why certain universal constraints on linguistic systems take the form that they do. In addition, they showed how the Marcus parser can be used to implement a psycholinguistically plausible model of language acquisition.

The publications just mentioned have aroused a good deal of attention for a variety of reasons. Some reseachers, most notably Frazier & Rayner (1982) and Fodor (1985), have questioned the psychological plausibility of the Marcus model. The main line of attack centres on the psycholinguistic implications of Marcus's hypothesis that the syntax of any natural language can be parsed strictly deterministically (the Determinism Hypothesis). Marcus's claims about the explanatory value of his model with respect to certain principles of grammar constitute another source of continuing debate. Finally, many computational linguists have expressed doubts as to whether any parser could realize a modern transformational grammar at all. Although there has been hardly any debate of this matter in publications (but see Berwick 1987, Wehrli 1984 and Johnson 1989), many seem convinced that principle-based grammars are impracticable from a computational point of view. This matter is less harmless than it seems, because it is intimately related to questions of psychological reality: if there exists no parser for some grammar G, then how can G be psychologically real?

Our investigation begins with a deep dive into the methodology underlying the development of representational theories of mind. What is the role of competence theories in the study of human cognitive abilities? Are they of any use in the development of computational theories of mind? Starting on familiar ground, we review the legitimacy of the competence-performance distinction in the study of natural language. We then sketch the contours of Marr's (1982) approach to the study of vision, which is in many ways similar to the Chomskyan research paradigm.

Then, having given extensive justification for the competence-performance distinction, we consider its implications for the notion of psychological reality. Because no two linguists ever seem to agree on what it means to say that some linguistic theory is psychologically real, an articulated view of this concept is developed first, which serves as a basis for the classification of grammar-parser correspondences that follows. Further, the question is raised whether there is a preferred relation between the grammatical theory and the parsing theory.

It is against this background that we discuss the Derivational Theory of Complexity and some of the developments in the field of linguistics that followed its failure. This historical survey finally brings into focus the Marcus parser and the last topic of the first chapter: what is a functional explanation and in what way does the existence of a functional explanation affect the grammar-parser relation?

In chapters 2 and 3 we turn our attention to a specific theory of grammar and a specific parsing model with the aim of performing a case study of a grammar-parser relation. In particular, we inquire into the explanatory potential of a Marcus-type parser with respect to current versions of transformational grammar.

Chapter 2 begins with an introduction into the Marcus model. After a discussion of the Determinism Hypothesis and the parser's rules and data structures, we counter some arguments against its lookahead buffer that have appeared in the literature. This is followed by a short discussion of modifications of the original Marcus parser that have been proposed by Berwick (1982,1985) and Berwick & Weinberg (1984).

We then examine in some detail the claim that a Marcus-type parser explains the existence of the Subjacency condition on overt syntactic movement. It will be shown that this claim is too optimistic. The most that can be made to follow from the Marcus parser, at least on the assumptions made by Marcus and Berwick & Weinberg, is the *Wh*-Island Condition.

We also argue against Berwick & Weinberg's claim that, given a GPSG grammatical framework, there is no functional derivation in terms of parsing for a constraint like Subjacency.

Finally, we discuss my (1987) attempt to provide a functional explanation for the version of Subjacency developed in Chomsky (1986a). The key idea in this paper was that a functional explanation of Subjacency should be impossible in the absence of a coherent characterization of the boundedness property. As Chomsky (op. cit.) provides a characterization of boundedness in terms of θ-marking, his revised version of Subjacency seemed a better candidate for functional explanation that of Chomsky (1973). We conclude that my attempt at functional explanation does not fare any better than Berwick & Weinberg's.

Chapter 3 switches to a more constructive mode. We begin by strengthening the relation between the competence grammar and the parser's grammar rules (the runtime grammar) by stripping the Marcus parser of linguistically unmotivated feature annotations. It will be shown that, as a consequence of this, the runtime grammar must allow unrestricted adjunction, because the parser enforces a very strong locality constraint on chain links. This analysis has a number of interesting consequences. To mention one: it reveals a deep parallel between violations of the *Wh*-Island Condition and cases of super-raising and super-passive.

The second part of chapter 3 develops a theory of deterministic chain formation. It is argued that, because several parsing problems that are quite common in natural languages require nondeterministic solutions, a strictly deterministic parser should incorporate ad hoc strategies to keep it from halting. The runtime grammar that emerges from this accords a central role to θ-marking in licensing chain links.

It will be shown that the proposed parsing model explains the existence of the Condition on Chain Links (Sportiche 1989), the Adjunct Condition, the Subject Condition and the non-existence of parasitic gaps licensed by a c-commanding trace. It can also be made to obey the *that*-trace filter in a rather interesting way.

Finally, in chapter 4, we ask whether the competence theory could profit from any of the insights that we have arrived at. This discussion brings together the results of our philosophical investigation and of our case study. We conclude that such insights are at best suggestive and require independent motivation at the level of the competence theory. If the insights gained from the parsing theory suggest modifications in the competence theory that are empirically neutral, then, to the extent that we have reasons to believe that the human sentence processor uses the particular algorithm that we have assumed, we should welcome these results, because, all other things being equal, we prefer the simplest possible relationship between the competence theory and the parsing theory.

Chapter 1

The Relation Grammar-Parser

1.1 Introduction

In this chapter we will be concerned with three intimately related questions. The first of these is: what legitimizes the distinction between competence and performance in the study of language? The answer to this question constitutes a cornerstone of the Chomskyan research paradigm. In section 1.2 we first review the methodological motivation for such a distinction, after which we show how Marr's (1982) *Vision* caused a breakthrough in the study of human visual perception by adopting a research paradigm very similar to that advocated by Chomsky.

Having firmly established the methodological justification for the competence-performance distinction, we address a second question: are there any a priori reasons to favour one grammatical theory over another simply on the grouds that it can be more transparently embedded in the particular parsing algorithm we have chosen? In other words: is there a preferred relation between the grammatical theory and the parsing theory? Over the years, and especially following the failure of the Derivational Theory of Complexity (Miller and Chomsky 1963, henceforth DTC), the grammar-parser relationship has been the subject of much heated debate. We follow the discussion of this complicated matter with a survey of possible grammar-parser relations. This survey is an attempt to characterize the possible relations between a grammar G of some natural language and a natural language parser P which is said to realize or *embed* G. Here we will draw rather heavily on work by Abney (1988). We also borrow some insights from chapter 2 of Berwick and Weinberg (1984).

Thus prepared, we embark on a short and undoubtedly incomplete survey of a number of important developments in the field of natural language parsing since the experiments carried out under the DTC first aroused attention. Each of these represents a particular view of the competence-performance distinction and of the relation between grammar and parser.

After this historical digression, we turn to the third question of this chapter: what is a functional explanation and how does the concept of functional explanation affect our view of grammar-parser relation?

1.2 The legitimacy of the competence-performance distinction

1.2.1 The mentalistic approach

What is a grammar? This question may be answered in a number of different ways, but for anyone underwriting linguistics as a mentalist discipline, the answer can only be: a grammar is a description of a speaker-hearer's competence, which consists of "a system of rules that in some explicit and well-defined way assign structural descriptions to sentences" (Chomsky,1965:p.8). Therefore, generative grammar is a mentalistic theory, "since it is concerned with discovering a mental reality underlying actual behaviour" (Chomsky,1965:p.4).

This view has been a continuing source of confusion ever since it was first expressed. Apparently, the warm reception transformational grammar was given by psychologists in the late fifties and early sixties was largely due to the misunderstanding that the mentalistic view implied that transformations could be considered active mental computations. Chomsky has not exactly been vague on this matter:

> "To avoid what has been a continuing misunderstanding, it is perhaps worth while to reiterate that a generative grammar is not a model for a speaker or a hearer. It attempts to characterize in the most neutral possible terms the knowledge of the language that provides the basis for the actual use of language by a speaker-hearer. When we speak of a grammar as generating a sentence with a certain structural description, we simply mean that the grammar assigns this structural description to the sentence. When we say that a sentence has a certain derivation with respect to a particular generative grammar, we say nothing about how the speaker or hearer might proceed, in some practical or efficient way, to construct such a derivation. These questions belong to the theory of language use - the theory of performance. No doubt, a reasonable model of language use will incorporate, as a basic component, the generative grammar that expresses the speaker-hearer's knowledge of the language; but this generative grammar does not, in itself, prescribe the character or functioning of a perceptual model or a model of speech production."
> (1965:p.9)

It would seem, then, that the interest in transformational grammar on the part of the psychology community did not generally extend to reading *Aspects of the Theory of Syntax*. The often heard allegation that many people were misled as a result of the suggestive terminology in the field cuts no ice: anyone who cared enough about generative grammar to read *Syntactic Structures* or *Aspects of the Theory of Syntax* could not possibly have been misled.

Despite its success, many have questioned the legitimacy of the study of competence. Yet the reasons for studying competence rather than performance are rather straightforward. Investigation of actual performance without prior successful investigation of competence is just too difficult: it cannot be done. In a nutshell the problem is that in language production and comprehension one's knowledge of language interacts with a wide variety of other factors, such as memory limitations, distractions, false starts, stylistic niceties and random errors. Therefore, to make serious inquiry possible at all, linguistic theory must be concerned with "an ideal speaker-listener, in a completely homogeneous speech-community, who knows its language perfectly" and who is unaffected by such performance limitations as just mentioned. Apart from just memory limitations, the idealization includes an abstraction from the procedures by which the human sentence processor puts grammatical knowledge to use. In section 1.3 and 1.5 we will consider more accurately the nature of this abstraction. For now, it suffices to note its methodological importance: since nothing of substance is known about the neural machinary involved in language processing, we could not construct a linguistic theory without this abstraction. For extensive discussion of these matters, I refer the interested reader to chapter 2 of Chomsky's *Knowledge of Language* (1986b). In what follows some familiarity will be presupposed with the methodological arguments bearing on this issue. We will relate the competence-performance distinction to the approach to the study of human visual perception developed by the late David Marr and his colleagues. The strong parallel between this research paradigm and the approach to the study of human linguistic abilities of the transformational school will allow us to rephrase the competence-performance distinction in terms of Marr's very precise explication of the structure of his approach. The comparison highlights the nature of some of the abstractions involved in the competence-performance distinction and lends additional support to its relevance and legitimacy.

1.2.2 Marr (1982)

The widespread unwillingness to accept the competence-performance distinction as a necessary prerequisite to the study of human linguistic abilities could very well be related to the happy circumstance that we are all so very good at language. Even today, many linguists are not at all ready to accept the view that the study of knowledge of language could require a level of abstraction similar to that in the exact sciences, that is, if it is to be an interesting discipline.

As Marr (1982) points out, researchers in the field of visual perception similarly held the belief that the study of vision lay in the domains of neurophysiology and psychophysics and until the early seventies no one had ever seriously considered developing a competence theory of visual perception[1]. In retrospect one can see how this situation developed. Early neurophysiological studies of the ganglion cells in the frog retina and numerous other single-cell studies that were conducted in the sixties suggested that a strong reductionist approach to the study of visual perception might be feasible. Marr cites Barlow (1972) to illustrate the point:

> "Neurons do not loosely and unreliably remap the luminous intensities of the visual image onto our sensorium, but instead they detect pattern elements, discriminate the depth of objects, ignore irrelevant causes of variation and are arranged in an intriguing hierarchy. Furthermore, there is evidence that they give prominence to what is informationally important, can respond with great reliability, and can have their pattern selectivity permanently modified by early visual experience. This amounts to a revolution in our outlook. It is now quite inappropriate to regard unit activity as a noisy indication of more basic and reliable processes involved in mental operations: instead, we must regard single neurons as the prime movers of these mechanisms. Thinking is brought about by neurons and we should not use phrases like "unit activity reflects, reveals, or monitors thought processes", because the activities of neurons, quite simply, are thought processes.
>
> This revolution stemmed from physiological work and makes us realize that the activity of each single neuron may play a significant role in perception."
>
> (p.380)

As Marr remarks, "the vigor and excitement of these ideas need no emphasis". He himself was fully caught up in the excitement, which at that time seemed justified. But in the course of the seventies the optimism gave way to dissatisfaction:

> "But somewhere underneath, something was going wrong. The initial discoveries of the 1950s and 1960s were not being followed by equally dramatic discoveries in the 1970s. No neurophysiologists had recorded new and clear high-level correlates of perception . . . None

---

[1]Marr uses the term *computational theory*, which is somewhat confusing, at least for linguists, who tend to associate the term *computational* with parsing. For Marr the distinction is between *computational* theory and *algorithmic* theory.

of the new studies succeeded in elucidating the *function* of the visual cortex.

It is difficult to say precisely why this happened, because the reasoning was never made explicit and was probably largely unconscious. However, various factors are identifiable. In my own case, the cerebellar study had two effects [Marr (1969) develops a theory according to which the simple and regular cortical structure is interpreted as a simple but powerful memorizing device for learning motor skills - jvdk]. On the one hand, it suggested that one could eventually hope to understand cortical structure in functional terms, and this was exciting. But at the same time the study has disappointed me, because even if the theory was correct, it did not much enlighten one about the motor system - it did not, for example, tell one how to go about programming a mechanical arm. It suggested that if one wishes to program a mechanical arm so that it operates in a versatile way, then at some point a very large and rather simple type of memory will prove indispensable. But it did not say why, nor what that memory should contain.

The discoveries of the visual neurophysiologists left one in a similar situation . . . As one reflected on these sorts of issues in the early 1970s, it gradually became clear that something important was missing that was not present in either of the disciplines of neurophysiology or psychophysics. The key observation is that neurophysiology and psychophysics have as their business to *describe* the behaviour of cells or of subjects but not to *explain* such behaviour. What are the visual areas of the cerebral cortex actually doing? What are the problems in doing it that need explaining, and at what level of description should such explanations be sought?" (pp.14-15)

It soon turned out that there were no easy answers to these questions. As is especially clear in the following passage, some of the problems encountered in machine vision are very similar to problems one faces in machine recognition of spoken language:

". . . in the 1960s almost no one realized that machine vision was difficult . . . the idea that extracting edges and lines from images might be at all difficult simply did not occur to those who had not tried to do it. It turned out to be an elusive problem: edges that are of critical importance from a three-dimensional point of view often cannot be found at all by looking at the intensity changes in an image. Any kind of textured image gives a multitude of noisy edge segments; variations in reflectance and illumination cause no end of trouble; and even if an edge has a clear existence at one point, it is as likely as not to fade out quite soon, appearing only in patches

along its length in the image. The common and almost despairing feeling of the early investigators like B.K.P. Horn and T.O. Binford was that practically anything could happen in an image and furthermore that practically everything did."
(Marr 1982:p.16)

In *Vision* Marr presents a theoretical framework for the study of visual perception. He argues that complex information processing systems must be understood at three distinct levels. Following Kashket (1988)[2], we will refer to this as the natural computation framework:

Natural Computation Framework
"At one extreme, the top level, is the abstract computational theory of the device [i.e. the competence theory - jvdk], in which the performance of the device is characterized as a mapping from one kind of information to another, the abstract properties of this mapping are defined precisely, and its appropriateness and adequacy for the task at hand are demonstrated. In the centre is the choice of representation for the input and output and the algorithm to be used to transform one into the other [i.e. the performance theory - jvdk]. And at the other extreme are the details of how the algorithm and representation are realized physically - the detailed computer architecture, so to speak [e.g. an IBM-compatible or a brain - jvdk]."
(pp.24-25)

These three levels of description are related, but only loosely. It is to be expected that this will be more generally the case in multi-level descriptions of complex systems. The reason for this is that a competence theory can usually be implemented in a variety of different ways and that a particular algorithm can often be physically realized in a number of alternative ways as well. Yet, although algorithms and mechanism may sometimes be empirically more accessible, it is the nature of the competence theory that is of prime importance from an information-processing point of view:

"The reason for this is that the nature of the computations that underlie perception depends more upon the computational problems that have to be solved than upon the particular hardware in which their solutions are implemented. To phrase the matter another way, an algorithm is likely to be understood more readily by understanding the nature of the problem being solved than by

[2]See Kashket (1987) for an illustration of how work on natural language processing can profit from the methodology of Marr's approach.

> examining the mechanism (and the hardware) in which it is embodied.
>
> In a similar vein, trying to understand perception by studying only neurons is like trying to understand bird flight by studying only feathers: it just cannot be done. In order to understand bird flight, we have to study aerodynamics; only then do the structure of feathers and the different shapes of birds' wings make sense . . ." (p.27)

As a concrete example, Marr discusses the fact that the particular form of the receptive fields of retinal ganglion cells and lateral geniculate neurons cannot be understood "just by studying their anatomy and physiology":

> "We can understand how these cells and neurons behave as they do by studying their wiring and interactions, but in order to understand *why* the receptive fields are as they are - why they are circularly symmetrical and why their excitatory and inhibitory regions have characteristic shapes and distributions - we have to know a little of the theory of differential operators, band-pass channels, and the mathematics of the uncertainty principle".
> (pp.27-28)

Marr's approach should sound very familiar to linguists in the field of transformational grammar. And just in case one does not feel quite sure yet that Marr is really talking about a distinction similar to the competence-performance distinction:

> "Failure to recognize [the] theoretical distinction between *what* and *how* also greatly hampered communication between the fields of artificial intelligence and linguistics. Chomsky's (1965) theory of transformational grammar is a true computational theory [i.e. a competence theory -jvdk] in the sense defined earlier. It is concerned solely with specifying what the syntactic decomposition of an English sentence should be, and not at all with how that composition should be achieved. Chomsky himself was very clear about this . . . but the fact that his theory was defined by transformations, which look like computations, seems to have confused many people. Winograd (1972), for example, felt able to criticize Chomsky's theory on the grounds that it cannot be inverted and so cannot be made to run on a computer; I had heard reflections of the same argument made by Chomsky's colleagues in linguistics as they turn their attention to how grammatical structure might actually be computed from a real English sentence.
>
> The explanation is simply that finding algorithms by which Chomsky's theory may be implemented is a completely different

> endeavour from formulating the theory itself. In our terms, it is a study at a different level, and both tasks have to be done." (pp.28-29)

Marr's book is first and foremost a demonstration of the importance of his competence theory to the study of vision. The 3-D model takes the problem of vision to be to derive an object-constant[3] representation of shape from images and divides this derivation into three representational stages. The first of these, the primal sketch is a representation of strictly local properties of the two-dimensional image on the retina (e.g. intensity changes). This representation is mapped into the 21/2-D sketch, which is a viewer-centred representation of the orientation and rough depth of the visible surfaces, and of discontinuities in depth and orientation. The 21/2-D sketch is mapped into the 3-D model, which provides an object-centred description of shapes and their spatial organization in terms of primitives that represent the volume of space that a shape occupies.

The competence theory of vision is a representational model designed with the exclusive goal of solving an information-processing problem. To readers with a linguistic background, this may seem mundane and uninspiring, but to most people working in the field of vision, and indeed to many people working in the broad field of artificial intelligence, Marr's approach meant a great shift of focus. His methodology could be summarized with the sentence "study the structure of the information-processing problem before you study the mechanism that could implement its solution". The general methodological trend in the field of AI is reflected in the numerous examples of mechanism-based approaches to information-processing problems. Such mechanism-based studies do not address an information-processing problem directly, but instead study the mechanism through which a solution to an information-processing problem might be implemented. To the extent that problem-solving research has been done:

> "[it] has for obvious reasons tended to concentrate on problems that we understand well intellectually but perform poorly on, like mental arithmetic . . . - all problems in which human skills are of doubtful quality and in which good performance seems to rest on a huge base of knowledge and expertise.
>
> I argue that these are exceptionally good grounds for *not* studying

[3]Object constancy in the output of our visual system is such a dominant characteristic that one tends to overlook it. What is meant by object constancy is that we can recognize objects no matter from which angle we look at them. So if an object is rotated in one's visual field, it is experienced as constant rather than as a sequence of unrelated objects, each of which must be recognized anew.

how we carry out such tasks. I have no doubt that when we do mental arithmetic we are doing something well, but it is not arithmetic, and we seem far from understanding even one component of what that something is . . . If one ignores this stricture, one is left with unlikely looking mechanisms whose only recommendation is that they cannot do something we cannot do."
(pp.347-348)

Marr's advice is to

"find problems that we can solve well, find out how to solve them, and examine our performance in the light of that understanding. The most fruitful source of such problems is operations that we perform well, fluently, and hence unconsciously, since it is difficult to see how reliability could be achieved if there was no sound, underlying method."[4]
(p.347)

The methodology advocated in the field of transformational grammar is very similar in many respects to Marr's approach to the study of vision. Just as Marr's competence theory of vision is concerned with specifying what are "the particular characteristics of the world that are made explicit during vision" (p.330), the competence theory "is concerned solely with specifying what the

---

[4]A similar point is made by Hofstadter (1985). He argues that the major question of AI is: "what in the world is going on to enable you to convert from 100,000,000 retinal dots into one single word *mother* in one tenth of a second?" And also "to understand the fluid nature of mental categories, to understand the invariant cores of percepts such as your mother's face, to understand the strangely flexible yet strong boundaries of concepts such as *chair* or the letter *a*" (p.633).

This is not to suggest that Hofstadter's and Marr's views on what is good AI research are generally compatible. In particular, Hofstadter does not seem to share Marr's appreciation of the importance of competence theories in developing models of cognition. To give an example that nicely illustrates this, Hofstadter praises Norman and Rumelhart's (1974) work on long-term memory as "different in flavour from mainstream AI work" because they are psychologists who are studying "genuine cognition" and "are not afraid to let their vision of how the *mind* works be inspired by research and speculation about how the *brain* works" (p.639). Marr judges their work as follows:

"Again the danger is that questions are not asked in relation to a clear information-processing problem. Instead, they are asked and answers proposed in terms of mechanisms - in this case the mechanism is called an "active structural network", and it is so simple and general as to be devoid of theoretical substance. Norman and Rumelhart may be able to say that such an "association" seems to exist, but they cannot say of what the association consists, nor do they say that to solve problem *x* (which we humans can solve) memory must be organized in a particular way; and that if this organization exists, certain apparent "associations" occur as side effects"
(Marr:p.349)

syntactic decomposition of an English sentence should be, and not at all with how that composition should be achieved". In both cases the design of algorithms that implement such theories is a different task than formulating the competence theory itself.

1.3 The competence-performance distinction and the concept of psychological reality

1.3.1 The common enterprise

We have seen that the competence-performance distinction lies at the heart of the successful inquiry into (at least) two human cognitive abilities. This is not to say, however, that studies of the same ability at different levels of abstraction should not be considered a common enterprise. As was pointed out by Marr, a theory at one level of the Natural Computation Framework may be only loosely related to a corresponding theory at one of the other levels. On the other hand, at least some relation between the three levels of description must obviously obtain if claims about the (psychological) reality of competence theories are to have any content. We would not, for instance, be satisfied with a natural language parser that assigned structures to sentences that the competence grammar does not generate (except, perhaps, partial structures to locally well-formed bits and pieces of ungrammatical sentences). This raises the question whether there is a preferred relationship between theories at each level of the Natural Computation Framework.

In *Knowledge of Language* Chomsky says about the relation between linguistics and the brain sciences:

> "We observed that it is a task for the brain sciences to explain the properties and principles discovered in the study of mind. More accurately, the interdependency of the brain sciences and the study of mind is reciprocal. The theory of mind [i.e. the competence theory -jvdk] aims to determine the properties of the initial state S_0 and each attainable state S_L of the language faculty, and the brain sciences seek to discover the mechanisms of the brain that are the physical realizations of these states. There is a common enterprise: to discover the correct characterization of the language faculty in its initial and attained states, to discover the truth about the language faculty. This enterprise is conducted at several levels: an abstract characterization in the theory of mind, and an inquiry into mechanisms in the brain sciences. In principle, discoveries about the brain should influence the theory of mind, and at the same time the abstract study of states of the language faculty should formulate properties to be explained by the theory of the brain and is likely to

> be indispensable in the search for mechanisms. To the extent that such connections can be established, the study of mind - in particular, of I-language - will be assimilated to the mainstream of the natural sciences."
> (pp.38-39)

As Chomsky hastens to point out, so little is actually known about the brain that we can do no more than speculate what the connections might be. About one thing he is very clear, however: all other things being equal, we should favour theories of mind that can be most transparently related to (theories of) the brain:

> "Suppose that theory I contains the principles $P_1,...,P_n$ and theory II contains the principles $Q_1,...,Q_m$, and that the two theories are logically equivalent: The principles of each can be deduced from the principles of the other so that any description of behavior or potential behavior in terms of one of these theories can be reformulated in terms of the other. It could be that the brain sciences would show that each P_i corresponds to some determinate complex of neural mechanisms, whereas there is no such account of the Q_i's; some brain injury, for example, might selectively modify the P_i's but not the Q_i's. In such a case, facts about the brain would select among theories of the mind that might be empirically indistinguishable in other terms. Although results of this sort are remote in the current state of understanding, they are possible. The relation of brain and mind, so conceived, is a problem of the natural sciences."
> (pp.39-40)

Some caution is required in interpreting Chomsky's words. The argument is that theory I is to be preferred over theory II on grounds of *simplicity*, not that theory II is *wrong*. Remember that both theories are competence theories and as such they abstract from implementation and hardware considerations. What Chomsky is arguing for is a maximally simple relation between the levels of description.

In order to appreciate the subtlety of the argument, let us conduct another simple thought experiment. Suppose we only have theory II, which contains the principles $Q_1,...,Q_m$. Theory I does not exist. An investigation into a wide range of brain damages reveals that there are no brain injuries that selectively modify any of the Q_i's (though perhaps always half of some Q_i and half of some Q_j in conjunction). Would this constitute experimental evidence that theory II is not psychologically real and therefore wrong? Clearly, the answer is no. There are no a priori reasons to expect a very transparent mapping between the Q_i's and neural mechanisms. What Chomsky is not arguing for, then, is the view that we should favor one theory of grammar over another *simply because it is more transparently realized in the brain*. The issue of simplicity becomes relevant if there are two "best" theories of grammar that are logically equivalent.

What emerges from these thought experiments is an articulated view of the concept of psychological reality: logically equivalent theories of UG may be ranked higher or lower on the scale of psychological reality depending on the complexity of the relation between each theory and its correspondent theories on the other levels of the Natural Computation Framework. In the following section we will be more explicit about what relations can in fact obtain between a competence theory and its corresponding parser.

1.3.2 Grammar-parser correspondences

Abney (1988) discusses four types of grammar-parser correspondence that have appeared in the literature, with the aim of giving formal content to claims about psychological reality. This section is a summary and a critical discussion of Abney's classification of grammar-parser correspondences. An attempt has been made to avoid technicalities where possible.

1.3.2.1 I/O Correspondence

The standard view of the grammar-parser relation in computational linguistics is that the parser is an *interpreter* (or *universal parser*) for a given grammar formalism. This is a particularly attractive view because it allows one to vary the grammar while keeping the interpreter constant. To see what is meant by an interpreter, it will help to consider a concrete example[5].

The so-called Earley algorithm (Early 1970) is the universal parser for the context-free grammar formalism. It is a very simple procedure that assigns structure to sentences by "walking through" the rules of a context-free grammar (henceforth CFG). A parse proceeds as follows. The parser consumes its input word by word. For every word, the parser builds a so-called *state-set*, which consists of a collection of *dotted rules*. A dotted rule is a rewrite rule with a dot somewhere in the righthand side of the rule indicating how many of the preterminals in that righthand side the parser has sofar encountered. Each word,

[5]The following explication of the Earley algorithm is an edited version of Abney's (op. cit.) short and simple description of its operation.

then, becomes associated with a state set that is an explicit representation of all possible legal parses of the input string seen sofar.

Let us quickly go through an example. Suppose we are parsing the context-free grammar below:

S → NP VP
NP → Det N
NP → N
VP → V NP
VP → V

We must first construct the initial state-set, which starts out with the special state: 0. Start → •S,0,$. This state must be read as "we are beginning the recognition of an S, and when we are finished with this rule, the next word in the input must be the end-of-input marker *$*". Because state 0 tells us that we must begin an S, we add all states to the initial state set that correspond to what is called *pushing* on S, i.e. we add all states corresponding to expansions of S. There is only one: 1. S → •NP VP,0,$. This state tells us that we must begin an NP, so we also push on NP, which gives us two more states:
2. NP → •Det N,0,V, and 3. NP → •N,0,V. Notice that the *lookahead symbol*, i.e. the preterminal that signals completion of the rule, is V in these states. This is because VP is the only phrase that can follow the NP, and V is the only preterminal that can legally begin a VP. Since both Det and N are preterminals, no other pushes are possible. State-set 0 therefore consists of the following states:

0. Start → •S,0,$
1. S → •NP VP,0,$
2. NP → •Det N,0,V
3. NP → •N,0,V161,25

Suppose the first word we read from the input is an N. We must now *shift* on N in state 3. This means that we must move the dot to the right of N in this state. Because we have now completed the expansion of the NP, we need only verify if the next word in the input is a V. Suppose it is. This gives us the first state of state-set 1: 4. NP → N•,0,V. Then we can *pop* NP, which means that we go back to state-set 0, where the rule NP → N was introduced, and shift on NP in any state looking for an NP. Since S → NP VP is the only rule in state-set 0 looking for an NP, we add to state-set 1 the state 5:
5. S → NP•VP,0,$. Because we now have a dot in front of VP, we must push

on VP, giving us two more states. This, then, is state-set 1 :

4. NP → N•,0,V
5. S → NP•VP,0,$
6. VP → •V NP,1,$
7. VP → •V,1,$

The parse continues in this way until a state set has been built for each word in the input. If the state Start → S•,0,$ is in the final state set, the sentence has been recognized as grammatical. The algorithm as we have discussed it only recognizes sentences as either grammatical or ungrammatical, but a simple modification suffices if one wishes to recover the parse of the sentence as well.

From this exposition it should be rather obvious that the Earley parser can be used to parse any CFG, i.e the Early parser is a universal parser for the context-free grammar formalism. It takes any grammar in the class of CFGs and becomes a parser for that grammar. In addition, it computes exactly the function specified by that grammar, which for Abney is precisely the relation between the grammar and the parser that is required by *Input/Output Correspondence* (henceforth I/O Correspondence).

We could, however, imagine a somewhat weaker relation between the grammar and the parser that would satisfy the requirements imposed by a slightly relaxed version of I/O Correspondence. In particular, we will also speak of I/O Correspondence if the parser computes a function $f_P \neq f_G$ (where f_G is the function specified by the grammar and f_P is the function specified by the parser), where there exists an effectively computable mapping Γ, such that $f_P(s)=\Gamma(f_G(s))$. That is, we require an effectively computable one-one mapping from structures computed by the parser to structures generated by the grammar. This relation is diagrammed below, where CG is the competence grammar of some particular language L, RG is the *runtime grammar* of L (i.e. the grammar that the parser uses online), and PE is a parsing engine for RG. We will henceforth carefully distinguish between PE (a parsing engine or interpreter for RG), and P (a parser, i.e. RG+PE):

(1) I/O Correspondence

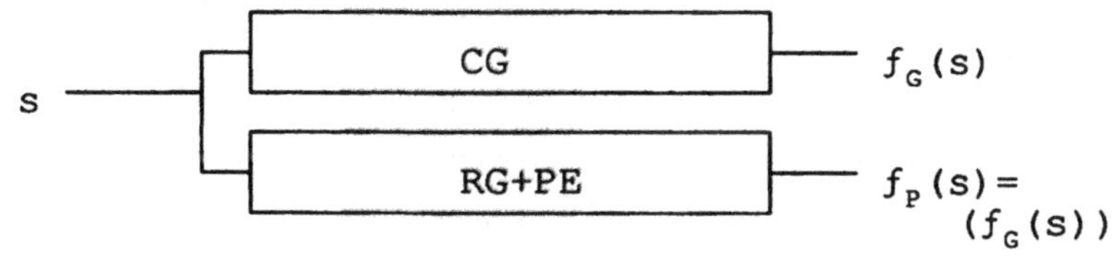

It should be noted that I/O Correspondence does not forge a tight relation between CG and RG. In particular, I/O Correspondence does not require that CG and RG be isomorphic. It is perhaps useful to point out that the Earley parsing engine is in fact rather exceptional in using its input grammar *online*, i.e. in using a version of its input grammar that has not undergone any translation. What is much more common is that the grammar interpreter translates (or *compiles*) the input grammar into a form that speeds up the parsing process. Abney gives an example that will be quite useful to us when we turn to the Marcus parser in the following chapter: for a subset of CFGs called LR grammars, it is possible to build very efficient parsers by compiling the input grammar into a special rule table. Such an LR rule table can be interpreted by an LR interpreter. Together, the LR table and the LR interpreter form an LR parser.

1.3.2.2 Degenerate I/O Correspondence

Even though I/O Correspondence does not require a tight relation between CG and RG, it does constrain the relation between CG and the parser P (i.e. RG+PE). Abney distinguishes a grammar-parser relation that is still weaker in that the function computed by the parser may differ from the function specified by the grammar in at least two ways. First, the structure that P assigns to sentences may differ from the structures that CG specifies, even though there must be a one-one mapping between them (we have just subsumed this case under I/O Correspondence). Second, there may be sentences to which CG, but not P, assigns a structure. Abney calls this relationship Weak Correspondence. He points out that Weak Correspondence is the sort of grammar-parser relation that Miller & Chomsky (1963) discuss in connection with the unacceptability of multiple centre-embedding[6]. Miller and Chomsky say that P *partially understands sentences in the manner of G* (p.468). To be precise, it understands

[6] Chomsky (1959,1963) discusses a method by which a finite state automaton (FSA) can be constructed for any non-centre-embedding context-free grammar.

sentences in the manner of G to the extent that the degree of multiple centre-embedding does not give rise to an overflow of the computing space available to P. Abney mentions a few other cases that might be classified as exemplifying Weak Correspondence, such as so-called garden path sentences like *the horse raced past the barn fell*, which are grammatical, but unparsable (at least, the first time one encounters them), and ungrammatical sentences, which are not assigned a structure by the grammar, while the parser presumably assigns some structure to locally well-formed parts.

There are good reasons for distinguishing between the two aspects of Abney's Weak Correspondence, which become at once apparent once we couch them in terms of Marr's Natural Computation Framework. The point is that the proposal to accommodate the unacceptability of multiple centre embeddings or garden paths by an appeal to memory limitations involves invoking properties of the lowest level in Marr's framework, i.e. the hardware level, in order to simplify the overall description of human linguistic behavior[7]. In particular, the contention is *that these phenomena can only be explained at this level.* To make this point a little clearer, consider Marr's remarks concerning analogous problems in the study of vision:

> "In attempts to relate psychophysical problems to physiology, too often there is confusion about the level at which problems should be addressed. For instance, some are related mainly to the physical mechanisms of vision - such as afterimages (for example, the one you see after staring at a light bulb) or such as the fact that any color can be matched by a suitable mixture of the three primaries (a consequence principally of the fact that we humans have three types of cones). On the other hand, the ambiguity of the Necker cube seems to demand a different kind of explanation. To be sure, part of the explanation of its perceptual reversal must have to do with a bistable neural network (that is, one with two distinct stable states) somewhere inside the brain, but few would feel satisfied by an account that failed to mention the existence of two different but perfectly plausible three-dimensional interpretations of this two-

[7]In the case of the unacceptability of multiple centre-embedding matters are in fact somewhat more complicated. The proposal to account for this phenomenon in terms of a particular parsing model (a finite state automaton) at first sight only invokes properties of the algorithmic level. This cannot be the end of the story, however. There is no reason why the finite state automaton could not be so large as to be able to parse sentences involving, say, centre-embeddings upto a depth of 30 sentences. To get the automaton to behave in a way similar to humans, we have to impose additional memory limitations that yield the effect that the automaton can only analyze cases upto 2 or 3 centre-embeddings. This brings the finite state proposal down to the hardware level.

dimensional image."
(Marr:pp.25-26)

Now although it can be rather easily imagined how an overflow of computing space could give rise to the unacceptability of multiple centre-embedding, it is quite inconceivable how the fact that P does not output a representation that is token-token identical to the representation generated by CG could be explained away by an appeal to properties of the hardware level. For this reason we reserve the grammar-parser relation Degenerate I/O Correspondence (D-I/O Correspondence for short) to designate failure on the part of the parser to compute a function that allows a one-one mapping to the function specified by the competence grammar.

Summarizing, we can say that in the case of D-I/O Correspondence CG and RG are I/O Correspondent, whereas CG and P are not because some property of the hardware in which PE lies embedded affects P's I/O behaviour:

(2) D-I/O Correspondence

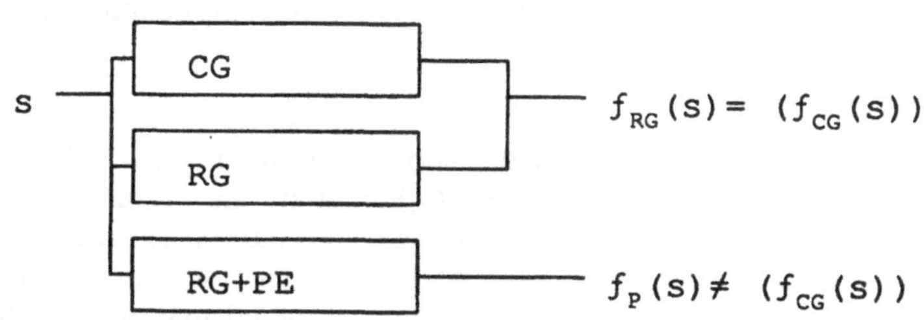

1.3.2.3 Strong Equivalence

As was pointed out in the discussion of I/O Correspondence, grammar compilation is a very common practice: not many grammar interpreters use their input grammar online. Yet, this is exactly the requirement imposed by *Strong Equivalence* (this is what Abney calls *Strong Correspondence*). For Strong Equivalence to obtain CG and RG must be *isomorphic*, i.e. if grammar compilers are used at all, they must perform only trivial mappings.

Now let us step back for a moment and consider how the notions D-I/O Correspondence, I/O Correspondence and Strong Equivalence are connected. Abney's discussion of these correspondences suggests, though perhaps unintendedly, that all fall in the category of *grammar-parser relations*. However, this classification is incoherent. D-I/O Correspondence and I/O Correpondence do fall in this category, because they compare the I/O mapping of CG with the I/O mapping of P, i.e. of RG+GE. Strong Equivalence, on the other hand, characterizes a particular relation between CG and RG and is completely neutral as to whether CG and P are I/O Correspondent or not. It is for this reason that I have decided to replace Abney's terminology. The distinction between correspondence and equivalence is necessary, because we could very well imagine a pair of grammars (CG,RG) that are Strongly Equivalent, while CG and P (which incorporates RG) are D-I/O Correspondent: for instance, an Earley parser with a limited memory tape[8]. In the following two subsections we will discuss two other grammar equivalences: Covering Equivalence and Metastrong Equivalence.

1.3.2.4 Covering Equivalence

"One grammar is said to *cover* another if the first grammar can be used to recover all the parses that the second grammar assigns to input sentences" (Berwick & Weinberg 1984:p.78). The relation of Covering Equivalence is the relation that we discussed earlier in terms of grammar compilation. As Berwick & Weinberg point out:

> "Informally, one grammar G_1 covers another grammar G_2 if (1) both generate the same language $L(G_1)=L(G_2)$, that is, the grammars are weakly equivalent; and (2) we can find the parses or structural descriptions that G_2 assigns to sentences by parsing sentences using G_1 and then applying a "simple" or easily computed mapping to the resulting output."
> (1984:p.79)

So, while Strong Equivalence implies a prohibition against grammar compilation, Covering Equivalence represents precisely the equivalence relation between CG and RG that obtains under grammar compilation.

1.3.2.5 Metastrong Equivalence

Like the other two equivalence relations, Metastrong Equivalence (Abney's Metastrong Correspondence) is completely neutral with regard to the I/O relation between CG and P (i.e. RG+PE). However, Metastrong Equivalence not only

---

[8]An example of such a truncated push down transducer appears in Krauwer and Des Tombe (1980).

forges a link of Strong Equivalence between CG and RG, in addition it requires PE to be a direct implementation of the semantics of the grammar (the *metasemantics*: hence the *meta* of *metastrong*). Abney explains:

> "A *theory of grammar T* is a specification of the syntax and semantics for a family of grammars *G(T)*. *T* consists of a *metagrammar*, which specifies which objects are well-formed grammars of *T* - i.e., which specifies the membership of *G(T)* - and a *metasemantics*, which assigns to each grammar *G* in *G(T)* its extension, f_G. For example, the context-free grammar formalism states that *G* is a well-formed grammar iff it is a 4-tuple (V_N, V_T, P, S), where V_N is a set of non-terminals, V_T is a set of preterminals, *S* is a start symbol drawn from V_N, and *P* is a set of rewrite expressions . . . , such that the lefthand side of every rewrite expression in *P* is of length one. The CFG metasemantics states that *G* assigns structure Σ to sentence *s* iff there is a derivation *d* of *s* from the start-symbol *S*, and Σ is the graph of *d*."
> (p.4)

We see then that under Metastrong Equivalence the grammar semantics constitutes a claim about the operation of PE, the parsing engine. Notice that, as with Strong Equivalence, we could very well imagine a Metastrongly Equivalent but D-I/O Correspondent pair (CG,P). For this situation to occur, PE would have to be a direct implementation of the semantics of the grammar, while PE+RG only partially understand sentences in the manner of CG, e.g. due to a limitation on the computing space available to PE.

1.3.2.6 Overview

In summary, we have six grammar-parser relations that can be classified along two dimensions (equivalence and correspondence). In particular, we have distinguished three equivalence and two correspondence relations.

In the following section we will survey some of the more important developments in linguistic theory that followed the negative results of the first investigations into psychologically plausible parsing models for transformational grammars. Especially the theoretical status of the three equivalence relations that we have discussed will be shown to have played a crucial role in the various developments in the field.

1.4 A historical survey

1.4.1 The Derivational Theory of Complexity

Research in the field of generative grammar has always aimed at answering the key psychological question of how people acquire their native language. But more than this, it was hoped that a transformational theory would point the way towards a theory of human sentence processing, the general idea being that the structures in which linguistic knowledge lies embedded (the grammar) form a natural basis for the way that knowledge is put to use (the parser). As will become clear shortly, these hopes were often founded on serious misinterpretations of the concerns of generative grammar.

The relationship between theories of grammar and theories of parsing was first investigated in the 1960s. Miller and Chomsky (1963) argued that experimental inquiry should start from the simplest position, assuming a one-to-one relation between rules and operations of the grammar and rules and operations of the parser. This is the relation between CG and P (i.e. RG+PE) that we have dubbed Metastrong Equivalence (Abney's 1988 Metastrong Correspondence). Remember that Metastrong Equivalence not only requires that the grammar be used online by the parsing engine, but in addition that the parser's operations are a natural implementation of the semantics of the grammar formalism (the metasemantics).

Abney argues that even though Metastrong Equivalence may be the simplest possible relation between grammar and parser, it is also the one that is least compatible with a competence-performance distinction of the sort proposed by Chomsky (1963) and Miller and Chomsky (1963):

> "Chomsky & Miller's reason for adopting Weak Correspondence is that we can simplify our linguistic descriptions by abstracting away from strictly performance issues such as the finiteness of human memory. The general issue is modularity of explanation: by treating separately the questions of the nature of language, and the processing of language, we can simplify our theory as a whole. The stronger types of correspondence, on the other hand, require one to address both questions simultaneously."
> (p.6)

This is only partly true, however. Although Metastrong Equivalence imposes very strong (and probably unrealistic) conditions on the design of the parser, for which there is no logical necessity, it leaves open the possibility of D-I/O Correspondence and hence of a performance account of unacceptability phenomena of the type exemplified by multiple centre-embedding.

In the Derivational Theory of Complexity (or the DTC) Metastrong Equivalence was adopted as a basis for calculating the psycholinguistic predictions of the Standard Theory of Transformational Grammar. The DTC consisted of three very simple hypotheses about the nature of human sentence processing.

The first of these was about what sort of representation the parser computed. Because the Standard Theory of Transformational Grammar (Chomsky 1965) was taken as the optimal theory of grammar, Metastrong Equivalence required the rules and operations of the parser to be an isomorphic mapping of the rules of the Standard Theory.

The second hypothesis concerned the way in which that representation was computed. It was assumed that the parser first constructed a surface structure on the basis of the phrase structure component of the grammar. It then applied inverse transformations in order to derive the underlying deep structure.

The third hypothesis was about the time cost associated with the parser's operations. This final hypothesis really consisted of two parts. First, every grammatical operation (i.e. every parsing analogue of a transformation) was assumed to have a unit time cost. That is, it was implicitly assumed that every operation takes exactly the same amount of time. Second, inverse transformations were assumed to apply serially only. In other words, the parser could not apply two grammatical operations at once. It is important for the reader to understand that, apart from the fact that transformations were partially ordered, nothing forced these assumptions. The serial nature of the parsing model was just one of a number of hypotheses underlying the investigation. We see then that according to the DTC the total time cost of a parse is simply the sum of the unit time costs of the parsing operations that have applied. Early work, done by McMahon (1963), Gough (1965) and Savin and Perchonock (1965) seemed to support the DTC but later experiments, especially those by Slobin (1966) and Walker et al. (1968) evidently disconfirmed it. It was concluded that "the grammar is probably not concretely realized in a perceptual model" (Fodor, Bever and Garrett 1974:369-370).

The results of the DTC experiments have often been construed as the final blow for transformational grammar as a psychologically plausible model of grammar. This was one of the reasons that in the late sixties and early seventies very many psychologists, but many linguists as well, turned their backs upon transformational grammar. But even a superficial survey of the hypotheses that the DTC set out to test immediately reveals that such dramatic conclusions were rather premature, to say the least. The apparent failure of the DTC to provide psycholinguistic support for the theory of grammar could have resulted in new attempts with a modified parsing algorithm (i.e. one could have weakened the equivalence relation) or with different assumptions about the time cost of particular parsing operations. Alternatively, one could have questioned the implicit assumption of strict seriality. Most alternative proposals, however, started from the position that transformational grammars cannot be successfully embedded in a parsing algorithm.

1.4.2 Lexical Functional Grammar

As we have just seen, one way to look at the DTC is as an attempt to adopt Metastrong Equivalence as a method for deriving psycholinguistic predictions from the competence theory. Metastrong Equivalence was just one of a number of possible hypotheses (in fact, the null hypothesis) about the relation between grammar and parser. Nevertheless, many researchers have taken the view that enough is known about this relationship to make experimental data important in the evaluation of competing grammars. Lexical Functional Grammar, introduced by Bresnan et al. (1978,1982), is an example of a research program that *presupposes* the view of the grammar-parser relation that we have dubbed Strong Equivalence: an isomorphic relationship between CG and RG. One of Bresnan's (1978) proposals is to remove all cases of syntactic NP movement from the grammar and from the parsing model. Instead, she reformulates these "active" computations as precomputed templates. This is done by associating a passive verb form in the lexicon with a functional template[9]:

Be + sing
(*y* [*y sing* NP_1 (*to* NP_3)])

In parsing a sentence with a passive verb form, the parser would now carry out exactly the same matching operation as in a sentence with an active verb. This arrangement allows Bresnan to embed the modified grammar in a parser that models the psycholinguistic facts by associating a unit time cost with each

[9]In a recent complexity theoretic study of the LFG framework, Barton, Berwick and Ristad (1987) show that the agreement machinary used in LFG's f-structure can be used to solve NP-hard problems (i.e., roughly speaking, problems that cannot be solved in less than exponential time on a deterministic computer, where the time complexity is a function of the size of the problem). They point out that the agreement machinary could be appropriately restricted by having the f-structure language obey X'-theory. Williams (1984) has made this suggestion for independent reasons. Interestingly, this restriction on LFG's f-structure representations would increase the similarity between LFG and Government Binding Theory. Perhaps, one might speculate, even to the point where the two treatments of displaced NPs could be shown to be notational variants.

"active" computation (the third DTC hypothesis). Bresnan claims that the compatibility of her grammar-parser pair with psycholinguistic data like Slobin's (1966) provides a strong reason for preferring her Extended Lexical Grammar over a transformational one[10].

The modifications in the grammar Bresnan has proposed constitute a fundamental departure from the Chomskyan view of grammars as models of linguistic competence, because they are based on the view that grammar rules correspond to actual mental operations[11]. Chomsky has pointed out time and again that the grammar does not specify *how* people actually compute sentences (which, by the way, goes to show that Chomsky only adopted Metastrong Equivalence as a null hypothesis). The grammar only specifies *what* the knowledge is that people have of their language. To equate transformations with active computations is to conflate two distinct theoretical levels, that of the competence theory and that of the algorithmic theory, into one. As we have seen in section 1.2, this is a questionable move from a methodological point of view.

Finally, consider Bresnan's claim that enough is known about the relation between grammar and parser to make experimental data important in the evaluation of competing grammars. It clearly does not hold up, since hardly anything of substance about this relation is known. Most of the things we do know about the human parser are due to the constraining power of the competence theory[12]. First, we know that some algorithms, like the Early algorithm, cannot parse a transformational grammar. Such algorithms may therefore be removed from the list of candidate algorithms. Second, the grammar specifies *what* knowledge must be represented. In some cases this may constrain the form of representations. For instance, since c-command is a predicate of the Government Binding Theory, the parser must somehow be able to compute it from the parsing representation. Third, the grammar may be taken to specify which primitives can play a role at the level of the parsing theory. An example of what I have in mind appears in Berwick and Weinberg (1984). There it is argued that natural grammars cannot "count" (a claim at the level of the

---

[10]In point of fact, an actual implementation of a transformational grammar could very easily be made to comply with the relevant psycholinguistic data (cf. Berwick and Weinberg 1984).

[11]Notice that this is a weaker view than that implied by metastrong equivalence. Under metastrong equivalence grammar rules not only mirror mental operations, but the grammar semantics also constitutes a claim about the nature of these operations.

[12]There are some notable exceptions. For instance, some researchers consider garden path phenomena an important indication about the nature of the human sentence processor.

competence theory) and that therefore parsing rules should not be allowed to count the number of bounding nodes intervening between a displaced constituent and its trace. Instead, they maintain that parsers may simulate a very rudimentary ability to count through the primitive notion of adjacency. We will return to this delicate matter several times in this work.

1.4.3 Generalized Phrase Structure Grammar

The original motivation for Generalized Phrase Structure Grammar (Gazdar 1979,1981) was a desire to eliminate the transformational component of the grammar entirely. This desire can be traced back to the important observation that the outputs of many of the transformations in the Standard Theory were identical to structures that could be generated by the base-component.

Proponents of GPSG have not generally been very explicit about their view of the relation between GPSG and human linguistic performance, except that some have argued that considerations of parsing efficiency could possibly restrict the class of possible grammars to the class of context-free grammars. The structure of this argument is rather simple. Any GPSG can be converted into a weakly equivalent context-free grammar. Since there exist fast algorithms for parsing context-free grammars[13], and since not all transformational grammars can be parsed rapidly, context-free grammars seem to have an important advantage over transformational ones:

> Suppose, in fact, that the permitted class of generative grammars constituted a subset of those phrase structure grammars capable of generating context-free languages . . . we would have the beginnings of an explanation for the obvious, but largely ignored, fact that humans process the sentences they hear very rapidly. Sentences of a context-free language are provably parsable in a time which is proportional to the cube of the length of the sentence or less (Younger (1967), Earley (1970)). But no such restrictive result holds for the recursive or recursively enumerable sets potentially generable by grammars which include a transformational component.
> (Gazdar,1981:155)

Berwick and Weinberg (1984) point out that Gazdar's argument that considerations of parsing efficiency could possibly restrict the class of possible grammars to the class of context-free grammars does not stick, because there

[13]Earley's algorithm (Earley 1970).

exist some strictly context-sensitive grammars that *can* be efficiently parsed. Therefore, the class of context-free grammars cannot be identified with the class of efficiently parsable languages. They add to this that it is certainly not true that all context-free languages can be efficiently parsed (the results can be found in Rosenberg 1967).

Matters are much more complicated than Gazdar's argument suggests. It is common in the complexity literature to express the relative time complexity of an algorithm as a function of the length of the input. So, for instance, context-free parsing is of cubic time complexity, i.e. of order n^3. There is, however, a second factor that contributes to an algorithm's time complexity: grammar size. Hence, the true time complexity of a context-free recognition algorithm is $k.f(|G|)n^3$, where k is a constant that we can ignore in our discussion, $f(|G|)$ is a function over grammar size and n is the length of the input. For the Earley algorithm the time complexity is $k|G|^2n^3$, i.e. proportional to the square of the grammar size and the cube of the length of the input sentence. As is shown in chapter 8 of Barton, Berwick and Ristad (1987), converting a GPSG into a weakly equivalent context-free runtime grammar produces an astronomical number of context-free rules. They observe that the mathematical complexity results are vindicated in practice:

> "Phillips and Thompson (1985:252) observe that in their parser based on the GPSGs of Gazdar (1982), "To expand the [GPSG] grammar completely . . . would be ridiculously wasteful of space and time. (the toy grammar of English we use with GPSGP [their parser], of 29 phrase-structure rules and four metarules, which expands to 85 rules, is equivalent to several tens of millions of context-free rules.)" Similarly, Shieber (1983:137) notes that typical post-Gazdar (1982) GPSG systems contain "literally trillions" of derived rules. In appendix B, we estimate that the GKPS grammar for English contains more than 10^{33} admissible local trees."
> (p.251)

As it turns out, $f(|G|)$ is a hyperexponential function that will dominate the complexity of the Earley algorithm for all inputs that can be written down in the universe:

> ". . . in the mathematical worst case, if a GPSG with 2 symbols recognized a given sentence in .001 second, a grammar with 3 symbols would recognize the same sentence in 2.5 hours, and a grammar with a mere 4 symbols could take at least 10^{63} centuries."
> (p.251)

What we learn from this is that for a very interesting class of sentences, namely the relatively short ones that we usually utter, the time complexity of the human parser may actually be dominated by the size of the grammar[14].

GPSG, as opposed to LFG, has not been developed in response to the DTC experiments. More than that, Gazdar himself has explicitly denied that computational considerations were the original motivation for formulating his theory[15]. At some point, however, Gazdar became aware of its potential computational import and adduced this property as independent motivation for his theory.

1.4.4 Performance grammars

Following the apparent failure of the DTC, many psychologists and members of the AI community (and a substantial number of linguists as well) have pursued "psychological" theories of language. Such theories have their roots in cognitive psychology or artificial intelligence and typically deny the need for a competence-performance distinction. They very often reject the autonomy thesis[16] (Chomsky 1957) as well. For researchers working in the field of transformational grammar, reading a paper in this branch of linguistics can be a shocking experience. Let me give two examples from the collection of papers *Talking Minds* (1984), edited by Bever, Carroll and Miller. The book has been divided into three parts: Philosophy and Linguistics, Psychology, and Computational Models. In the psychology section Kintsch remarks:

> "If a cognitive theory is a representation-process pair, then it makes no sense to isolate competence. One can take note of a theory of competence as an intellectual achievement, but it is hard to discover the relevance of such a theory to the kinds of problem of interest here. A rejection of the competence-performance distinction, however, does not imply a rejection of linguistics; although linguistics-as-the-study-of-competence may be irrelevant for our purposes [formulating a processing theory-jvdk], much of linguistics is needed as a basis for cognitive science, for example,

---

[14]Conversely, a reasonably small context-sensitive grammar with a recognition algorithm of complexity $k.f(|G|)2^n$ (i.e. exponential time complexity) could still be quite efficient for inputs of moderate lengths.

[15]See Berwick and Weinberg (1984:p.87,fn.1.).

[16]The autonomy thesis holds that the set of grammatical sentences in a language L cannot be identified (i) with any particular finite corpus of utterances in L, or (ii) with the set of meaningful sentences, or (iii) in terms of a statistical model of grammaticalness.

> textlinguistics."
> (p.135)

First of all, competence theory is not *part of a representation-process pair*, as should by now be rather self-evident. Although it is quite conceivable that the correct competence grammar and the correct runtime grammar (whatever those may turn out to be) are Strongly Correspondent, there is no logical necessity for this type of grammar-parser relation. Yet, Kintsch seems to take that for granted.

In the computational models section Schank and Birnbaum suggest that the autonomy thesis implies that semantic processing cannot begin until the syntactic analyzer has built a complete structure:

> "In the mid-sixties, most linguists took syntactic phenomena as the relevant linguistic phenomena, and hence linguistic theory was essentially syntactic theory. The assumption was that there could be a "theory of syntax".
>
> At the root of this assumption was the distinction between competence and performance. Without this distinction, the attempt to construct a "theory of syntax" would have seemed quite problematic (which is not to say that the distinction is itself unproblematic). No one can seriously propose that people must, or even can, perform a complete syntactic analysis before they begin to decode the meaning of what they hear. Such a proposal seems dubious simply on introspective evidence. If we stop at any point in the course of understanding a sentence, we will find that we have already understood quite a bit of this only partially completed sentence, and that we have generated a great many expectations, based on meaning and world knowledge, about what the rest of the sentence might contain. Clearly, we do not wait for a complete syntactic analysis before we begin to process for meaning".
> (pp.209-210)

This critique of "the theory of syntax" is quite unjustified, however. The autonomy thesis is a claim about the nature of the competence theory. It was never intended as a claim about the logical structure of language processing.

But their rejection of the autonomy thesis even holds up under the correct interpretation of the thesis:

> "Research aimed towards elucidating a competence theory of syntax . . . naturally starts by deemphasizing the relationships between meaning and syntax. This methodological decision has in turn often led to psychological claims for various forms of *autonomous syntax*, most clearly seen in the work of Chomsky and others of the

> interpretive school. These claims have often been made without consideration of the kind of relationship between semantics and syntax that might be required in order to actually perform significant language-processing tasks. In research on artificial intelligence, however, this lack of attention to processing is simply impossible . . . What do our current [AI] theories say about the roles of memory, meaning, and syntax in language processing? Our working hypothesis is that meaning and world knowledge are often crucial even at the earliest points in the process of understanding language. We call this position the *integrated processing hypothesis*. As we shall see, this hypothesis stands in direct opposition to theories that posit a logically autonomous syntactic analysis procedure, preceding and providing input for, semantic processing."
> (p.212)

We see then that this approach to natural language processing divorces itself from the very foundations of mainstream linguistic theorizing.

1.4.5 Parsifal (Marcus 1980)

The publication of *A Theory of Syntactic Recognition for Natural Language* (Marcus 1980) marked the beginning of a renewed interest in parsing on the part of linguists working in the field of transformational grammar. After the apparent failure of the DTC to provide psycholinguistic support for the theory of transformational grammar, Marcus's work suggested that such theories could be concretely realized in a perceptual model after all.

What is particularly striking about Marcus's work is its methodology, which is very much that advocated by Marr. Marcus makes a serious attempt to give grammar-independent motivation for the parsing algorithm he assumes. The relationship between Parsifal's grammar[17] and the grammatical theory that he assumes, which is a post-Extended Standard Theory[18] pre-On Binding[19] grammar (henceforth EST and OB) that includes trace theory, is no stronger than Covering Equivalence. Although the function that Parsifal's runtime grammar computes is exactly the function specified by the grammar, i.e. no one-one mapping is necessary, CG and RG are not Strongly Equivalent. The actual rules and operations of the Marcus parser are in no sense direct translations of the

---

[17]Parsifal is the name that Marcus has given to his parser.

[18]Chomsky (1972).

[19]Chomsky (1980).

rules and grammar organization of transformational grammar. Still, the parser implements the competence grammar in the sense that it observes its constraints and builds representations that are transparently related to the representations it generates.

Interestingly, CG and Parsifal as a whole (i.e. RG+PE) are D-I/O Correspondent. In particular, there are grammatical sentences that Parsifal cannot parse. An example is a so-called garden path sentence, such as *the horse raced past the barn fell.* We will discuss Parsifal in some detail in the next chapter.

1.5 The relation grammar-parser and so-called functional explanations

1.5.1 Fodor's (1985) classification of functional explanations

A major part of this work is concerned with what are known in the parsing literature as functional explanations of grammatical principles. It is therefore perhaps worthwhile to consider this notion in the theoretical context outlined above. However, before we do that, we will first consider a three-way classification of functional explanations developed by Fodor (1985), to get a good impression of how this notion is used in the literature on natural language processing.

In her critique of Marcus (1980) and Berwick and Weinberg (1984), Fodor distinguishes three types of functional accounts, ranging from mere stipulation to true explanation of a linguistic constraint C by a parser P. All through the discussion that follows, the reader should bear in mind that Fodor does not distinguish between CG and RG. Instead, she uses the term *parser* (P) to refer to what we have called the parsing engine (PE) and the term *grammar* to refer to the runtime grammar (RG).

The weakest possible explanatory relationship between P and a linguistic constraint C (i.e. C is part of RG) that Fodor distinguishes is

> ". . . that P can be made to obey C, i.e., that the parameters of P can be set in such a way that it will not in fact parse sentences which violate C. This ability of P to *incorporate* C will provide support for P relative to other kinds of parsers only if the other kinds of parsers cannot be made to incorporate C (for instance, if C can only be formulated in terms of some property of sentences that these parsers are incapable of representing). P would then explain the existence of C in natural languages in the weak sense that if the human parsing mechanism did not share the relevant properties of P, C could not even be respected during parsing."
> (p.4)

Fodor calls this a type 1 functional account. She refines this type of account as follows:

> "Within this line of argument, we might want to make some further distinctions. For example, can P be made to incorporate C only by not allowing P to employ a grammar that doesn't include C? Or can it made to incorporate C by making it unable to compute structures that violate C even if these structures are compatible with the grammar it employs? The latter case would come closer to what is generally thought of as a functional explanation of the linguistic facts."
> (p.4)

The second case discussed here is virtually identical to what we have referred to as D-I/O Correspondence. In particular, if the second case obtains, then the function computed by P is not identical to the function specified by RG.

Fodor argues that a somewhat stronger claim about the explanatory relationship between P and a linguistic constraint C would be that P operates more efficiently if it incorporates C. She calls this a type 2 functional account. Although Fodor does not labor this point, exactly the same further distinctions that could be made for a type 1 functional account could be made here as well.

Fodor's definition of a type 3 functional account is that C is entailed by the defining properties of P. She adds:

> "This would be the strongest claim of all, but here too we might want to ask some further questions. For example, it would not be very impressive to show that the defining properties of P entail C if C were explicitly listed among those defining properties, for that would effectively reduce the account of C to a Type 1 account, in which case C is simply stipulated. To qualify as an explanation of C, the definition of P must apparently entail C "indirectly" in some sense that is not easy to pinpoint.
>
> We would also be unimpressed if C were shown to follow from the interaction of a great many different defining properties of P which seem to have been selected precisely so that C should follow, i.e. where each one could just as well have been replaced by its opposite, as far as any facts other than C are concerned. It would be particularly important in this case to give some reasons for believing that the human sentence parsing mechanism has exactly this complex of properties. In other words, we would recognize explanatoriness to the extent that the relevant properties of P are independently motivated in some fashion.
> (p.5)

In the following section we will critically examine Fodor's classification and develop an alternative classification that takes into account the level of competence theory.

1.5.2 Explanations of properties of the competence level at the algorithmic level: efficiency and strategy

The first half of Fodor's type 1 account (i.e. P abides by C) can be stated in our terms as the requirement that P (i.e. RG+PE) does not assign structures to sentences that CG does not generate. We can therefore reinterpret this notion of *functional account* as an attempt to define a minimal grammar-parser correspondence: everything is fine as long the function computed by P is a subset of the function specified by CG but still rich enough to account for the performance of humans. If the function computed by P is a superset of the function specified by CG and P cannot be appropriately constrained to remedy this, then P is not a parser for CG. In addition, if there exists no parser for CG, then CG cannot be psychologically real. The requirement that all linguistic constraints have this weak type 1 account is trivially implied in the Natural Computation Framework.

More interesting cases of type 1 accounts (let us refer to these as strong type 1 accounts) involve a D-I/O Correspondent relationship between RG and P: PE can be made unable to compute structures that are compatible with the runtime grammar, even though the properties of PE that give rise to this behavior are perhaps rather ad hoc. Whether or not this results in a D-I/O Correspondent relationship between CG and P is up to the linguist. In some cases, e.g. centre-embedding, it may be undesirable to state the relevant constraint in CG, while the opposite may be true in other cases. Suppose, for instance, that we had a strong type 1 account for certain subcases of a more general constraint C (C in CG). In such a case we would have a strong type 1 account and I/O-Correspondence.

A type 2 functional account of a linguistic principle C consists of an argument to the effect that P operates more efficiently because it incorporates C. Fodor puts it this way: if P were to operate more efficiently because of C, "[t]hen the claim that P incorporates C would not be entirely *ad hoc*." Now observe that the claim that some linguistic constraint C exists so as to facilitate the task of P is completely incoherent in the absence of auxiliary assumptions about evolutionary pressures that the human species has been exposed to. In particular, it must be shown that evolutionary pressure has resulted in the development of genetic material causing the growth of efficient parsers in members of the human species. The idea behind this claim is that properties of the human parser can be explained in terms of the communicative function of language. Unfortunately, there are no obvious evolutionary considerations that provide evidence that communication is the function of the human parser.

More generally, considerations of efficiency will not provide independent motivation for the fact that P (weak type 2) or PE (strong type 2) incorporates a constraint C, unless it can be established on independent grounds (e.g. evolutionary considerations) that a good parser is an efficient one.

For an illuminating discussion of a related issue see Koster (1982), who points out that the fact that language is *used* for communication does not mean that that is its function. Koster cites the Dutch author Van het Reve, who puts the matter poignantly as follows:

> "The statement that the function of the molars is to grind our food is no more reasonable than the thesis that the function of pigs is to supply us with chops. Everybody laughs about that statement by Pangloss, but everybody believes that story about molars."
> (From: *Een dag uit het leven van de reuzenkoeskoes* (p.23) by Karel van het Reve, my translation from Dutch - jvdk)

Needless to say, efficiency arguments for the existence of some linguistic principle C would certainly acquire credibility if it could be shown that genes responsible for an inefficient parser have less chance of being carried than genes that cause the development of an efficient parser in a human being. Unfortunately, one would also have to prove that the class of parsers parsing grammars of type X with C has better efficiency properties than the class of parsers parsing the grammars of type X without C. Abney (personal communication) points out that such proofs are much harder and usually require techniques from formal parsing theory.

Fodor's type 3 functional account entails that one must show that C is entailed by the defining properties of the parsing engine PE. Now, assuming that she is not referring to hardware properties of PE, what she must have in mind is an explanation of C in terms of the nature of the *strategy* that PE instantiates. As will become clear in the following chapters, constructing such an argument is exceedingly difficult. Apart from that, for the argument to have real force, one must provide independent motivation for PE. If one cannot do that, functional "explanations" remain dependent upon assumptions about the nature of PE that cannot be independently motivated.

1.5.3 Explanations of properties of the competence and algorithmic levels at the hardware level

The Natural Computation Framework's third source of explanation is the hardware level. We will refer to this type of explanation as hardware explanation. Here we can be very short: currently, nothing of substance is known about the neural machinary underlying the language faculty. The only attempts at hardware explanation that one sometimes comes across typically give rise to D-I/O Correspondence, and these therefore do not belong in the category considered here[20].

1.6 Conclusion

In this chapter we have explored the Natural Computation Framework of Marr (1982), which models complex information processors by describing them at three levels: (i) competence theory, (ii) representation and algorithm, and (iii) hardware. Central to this approach is the thesis that questions must be asked in relation to a clear information-processing problem, because it is first and foremost the abstract structure of the problem that determines the form of the algorithm. Therefore, the Natural Computation Framework accords a prominent role to competence theories in AI models of cognitive functions.

We have also developed criteria by which we can evaluate the logical connections between the levels of the Natural Computation Framework. We have seen that there are no a priori reasons to expect a very tight relationship between the levels, even though, all other things being equal, we clearly prefer the simplest possible relationship.

Finally, we have discussed the place of several types of explanation in this framework.

[20]The typical example would be memory overflow with multiple centre-embedding.

Chapter 2

Explaining Subjacency: An Overview

2.1 Introduction

Marcus's 1980 book *A Theory of Syntactic Recognition for Natural Language* was the first sign of renewed interest in developing a parsing model for a transformational grammar. This work suggested that, contrary to what many had concluded after the experiments with the DTC, such theories could be concretely realized in a perceptual model after all.

In this chapter we will first make ourselves familiar with the main features of the Marcus parser, also known as Parsifal. We discuss its data structures and rule types and some of the natural language phenomena that Marcus claims it accounts for. We then turn to a fairly lengthy discussion of the parser's so-called lookahead buffer, which has been claimed by several researchers to give rise to psycholinguistically false predictions. We will adduce several facts and arguments showing that this criticism is misguided.

In section 2.5 we discuss a number of modifications in the original Marcus parser that have been proposed by Berwick and Weinberg (1984), after which we take up the important matter of the explanatory value of Marcus's Determinism Hypothesis in section 2.7. Both Marcus and Berwick & Weinberg have claimed that certain properties of grammatical axioms can be derived from the formal properties of the (strictly) deterministic parsers they propose. Marcus's central claim is that a strictly deterministic model of the human sentence parsing mechanism provides functional explanations for the existence of otherwise unexplained constraints of the theory of grammar that he assumes (Marcus draws on material in Chomsky (1973,1977) and Chomsky & Lasnik (1977)). Similarly, it is claimed by Berwick & Weinberg that a parser of the type proposed by Marcus (which they assume is a so-called Bounded Context Parser) explains the existence of Subjacency. We will carefully dissect the logic behind their functional explanation of this locality constraint, showing that more modest claims would have been appropriate.

Finally, we review the attempt at functional explanation of Subjacency in Van de Koot (1987). We point out a number of shortcomings in the proposal and show that it relies on properties of the parser that cannot be motivated independently of the grammr.

2.2 The Marcus parser

2.2.1 The Determinism Hypothesis

Any computer program can be divided into a data structure and a process structure. The process structure is a collection of actions that manipulate and expand the data structure. As was explained in section 1.3.2, the process structure of a parser consists of a runtime grammar and a parsing engine. It stands to reason that the parsing engine (or *grammar interpreter*) must "know" when to execute which rule of the runtime grammar. This is generally taken care of by associating each rule (or *action*) with one or more conditions that constrain its application. Such a set of conditions consists of a description of the input and the internal state of the program. Thus, the execution of a particular rule is contingent upon the existence of a particular input configuration and a particular internal state.

Now imagine a situation in which the data structure is locally ambiguous. We will say that a sentence is *locally ambiguous* if it contains one or more words that are ambiguous in isolation but unambiguous in their context. A local ambiguity will give rise to serious problems, because it means that more than one action can apply. The parsers needs to resolve this conflict or it will halt. It would of course be very exciting if computers contained magic oracles telling them which action to execute. Unfortunately, computer oracles do not exist, except in the minds of computer scientists. Such (non-existent) oracle solutions are referred to as nondeterministic solutions, because in cases of local ambiguity the execution of an action is not uniquely determined by the input and the internal state of the program.

Clearly, since oracles do not exist, computers are deterministic. It is possible, however, to simulate nondeterministic solutions on deterministic computers by means of backtracking or parallel processing. In the case of backtracking, the program is constructed in such a way that it orders its hypotheses about the input and then tests each hypothesis against the input string in turn. The program accepts the input if one or more of its hypotheses lead to a success state. Alternatively, the program could pursue all alternative hypotheses in parallel. Here, too, we say that the program accepts the input if one or more alternative pathways lead to a success state.

The Marcus parser is deterministic in the nontrivial sense that it uses neither backtracking nor parallel processing to simulate nondeterministic operation. Marcus uses the notion "strict determinism" to refer to this much narrower concept and we will follow this practice here.

The Marcus parser has been developed on the basis of the Determinism Hypothesis, which holds that "the syntax of any natural language can be parsed by a mechanism which operates *strictly deterministically* in that it does not simulate a nondeterministic machine" (Marcus, 1980:2). Hence, every action of the Marcus parser is completely determined by its input and its internal state. As we have just seen, this means that it cannot make "guesses" about the proper sequence of actions for a given input: the Marcus parser (i) builds only one syntactic tree representation of a sentence[21], and (ii) it cannot withdraw previous decisions about the structure of sentences.

The Determinism Hypothesis is a very strong hypothesis indeed, as there are many syntactic constructions that seem to require nondeterministic parsing techniques. The examples below (Marcus, 1980:2) illustrate this point:

(1) (i) Is the block sitting in the box?
(ii) Is the block sitting in the box red?
(2) (i) Have the students who missed the exam take the makeup today.
(ii) Have the students who missed the exam taken the makeup today?

In the sentences (1i,ii) the status of the word *sitting* cannot be determined until the parser has seen whether the words following *sitting in the box* can serve as the predicate of the matrix clause. In (2i) *have* is the main verb of an imperative sentence, whereas in (2ii) *have* is the auxiliary of the main verb *taken*. The first seven words of these sentences are identical, however. In both (1) and (2) the disambiguating information appears to be inaccessible at the point where the ambiguity arises. After all, the parts of these sentences that contain the disambiguating material have not yet been analyzed.

Before we discuss how Parsifal deals with these problems, we must first say a little bit more about the Determinism Hypothesis itself. Marcus finally settles on what he calls a "psychological" formulation of the hypothesis, which runs as follows: "all sentences which people can parse without conscious difficulty can be parsed strictly deterministically" (Marcus 1980:p.6). It should be noted that this hypothesis differs from a version that maintains that all sentences generated by competence grammars can be parsed strictly deterministically. The psychological version credits one of the results that Marcus claims for his model: just like the human sentence processor, Parsifal runs into serious trouble with so-called garden path sentences like *the horse*

[21]Note that the definition of strict determinism might very well have been different in that it could have required the parser to be nondeterministic in the nontrivial sense that it should build all and only the correct syntactic representations for a given input.

raced past the barn fell[22]. Marcus's claim may therefore be construed to imply the following: if we assume that the human parser is strictly deterministic, then we predict the existence of a class of sentences which people cannot parse without conscious difficulty. Consider the sentences below (Marcus:fig.9-1,p.202):

(3) (i) The grocery store always orders a hundred pound bags of sugar.
(ii) I told the boy the dog bit Sue would help him.
(iii) The horse raced past the barn fell.

Parsifal gets "stuck" in these sentences at the point at which people become conscious they have been misled. Marcus claims that it runs into difficulties because these sentences contain a local structural ambiguity that cannot be diagnosed by a grammar rule that can only examine up to three lookahead cells[23]. In addition, he claims that the opposite holds true as well: local ambiguities that can be analyzed by a diagnostic rule with a three cell pattern do not give rise to garden path effects. We will review these claims below.

2.2.2 The data structures

Marcus shows that a deterministic parser must meet three basic criteria in order to be able to parse natural languages.

First, it must be at least partially data driven. That is, its actions must be partly determined by the input. This is immediately clear from the examples below:

(4) (i) John went to the store.
(ii) Did John go to the store?

A purely hypothesis driven (i.e. top-down) parser would fail on (one of) such simple examples as these. The reason for this is that such a parser must either hypothesize that the input sentence is a declarative, in which case it would fail on (4ii), or that the input sentence is a question, in which case (4i) cannot be parsed without failures.

On the other hand, deterministic parsing must be partly hypothesis driven as well, as the parser must be able to reflect expectations based upon properties

[22]We will discuss this claim later on this chapter.

[23]Diagnostic rules will be discussed below.

of the partial structures built up during a parse. Marcus gives the following example:

(5) (i) I called [$_{NP}$ John] [$_{IP}$ to make Sue feel better]
(ii) I wanted [$_{IP}$ John to make Sue feel better]

The different complementation structures of these two sentences can be readily predicted by the parser if we allow it to inspect the subcategorization frames associated with the preceding verbs[24].

Finally, the parser must have some sort of lookahead facility if we want it to correctly analyze such examples as in (6), where we have an imperative in (6i) and a yes/no-question in (6ii):

(6) (i) Have [$_{IP}$ the boys take the exam today]
(ii) Have [$_{NP}$ the boys] [$_{VP}$ taken the exam today]

The Marcus parser uses two very simple data structures from which it derives these properties. It has access to part of the representation of the parse tree under construction, the *Active Node Stack*, which is its *left context*. A stack is a last-in-first-out memory device and as such very well suited to deal with the recursive properties of natural languages. A finite automaton[25] that uses a stack is called a pushdown automaton. Pushdown automata use their stack to store information for later recall. It is this ability that distinguishes pushdown automata from finite state automata and gives them the ability to recognize context-free languages. As a simple example, consider the formal language example below together with the grammar that generates it:

[24]We discuss some of the problems caused by ambiguous subcategorization later on in this chapter.

[25]A finite state automaton is a device that can be in any of a finite number of states, one of which is an initial state and at least one of which is an accept state. Attached to this device is an input tape on which symbols from a given alphabet arrive in sequence. The machine has a tape head which gives it the ability to read the symbols as they arrive. Based on the current state and the symbol received, it exexutes a transition that either consists of switching to a new state or remaining in the current state. Exactly which transition occurs is determined by a control mechanism within the machine that is programmed to know what the new state should be, given the current state and the symbol read.

$L(G)=x^n y^n$ (n >= 0)
G: S → xSy
S → λ (where λ denotes the empty string)

L(G) is the language consisting of all strings consisting of some number of *x*'s (possibly zero) followed by an equal number of *y*'s. We distinguish between pushdown automata with a top-down strategy and pushdown automata with a bottom-up strategy.

A pushdown automaton that uses a top-down strategy could classify strings as belonging to the language L(G) or not in the following way. Starting from its initial state, it first pushes a bottom of stack marker onto the empty stack, e.g. the symbol #, while moving to a new state[26]. It then pushes the grammar's start symbol *S*, again moving to a new current state. From there, until the symbol # returns to the top of the stack, the automaton will either pop a nonterminal from the stack and replace it with the righthand side of an applicable rewrite rule, or it will pop a terminal from the top of the stack while reading the same terminal from the input. When the bottom of stack marker # returns to the top of the stack, the automaton will shift to its accept state, indicating that the input consumed thus far is acceptable. Suppose we give this automaton a string consisting of more *x*'s than *y*'s as input. Then it will not be able to empty its stack and therefore not accept the string. If, on the other hand, there are more *y*'s than *x*'s, the automaton will enter its accept state before it has read the entire string.

Pushdown automata with a bottom-up strategy are usually referred to as shift-reduce automata, after the names of the two primitive actions they perform. A *shift* removes the first symbol from the input and pushes it onto the stack. A *reduce* pops a string of terminal and/or nonterminal symbols corresponding to the righthand side of a rewrite rule from the stack and replaces this string with the corresponding lefthand side of the rule. A shift-reduce automaton parses strings from our example language as follows. After having marked the bottom of its stack with the special marker #, it shifts all *x*'s onto its stack. It then uses the second S-rule (S -> λ) to perform a reduce. This may seem a somewhat strange reduce, as nothing seems to be popped from the stack, but this just happens to be the case of popping the empty string. After it has shifted a *y* onto the stack, the automaton uses its first S-rule (S -> xSy) to perform a reduce on the string *xSy* that now forms the top of the stack. The result is a

[26]One usually thinks of the stack as a pile of symbols growing upwards. Putting a symbol on the stack is called a push, taking a symbol off the stack is called a pop.

new *S* on the top of the stack. The next shift again results in the string *xSy* appearing at the top of the stack, and hence another reduce follows. This chain of alternative shifts and reduces continues until one of the following situations obtains: (i) All input has been read (i.e. shifted onto the stack) and the start symbol of the grammar is sitting at the bottom of the stack. The automaton pops the *S* and the bottom of stack marker # and moves to an accept state; (ii) All input has been read and there are one or more *x*'s on the stack. Therefore, the bottom of stack marker cannot be popped and the automaton does not accept the input; (iii) The stack contains the symbols *Sy* (i.e. there were more *y*'s than *x*'s in the input) and the parser halts in a non-accept configuration.

Returning now to the Marcus parser's stack, we will see that it differs from standard automata in that it uses its stack to build explicit tree structure. Furthermore, it combines top-down and bottom-up operations. As will be explained in more detail in the next subsection, each constituent in the stack will have one or more sets of grammar rules (called rule packets) associated with it. Of these packets, only the ones associated with the top node in the stack (the Current) are active. Such active packets of rules reflect the parser's expectations. Following Marcus, we will conceive of the stack as growing *downward*, so that the structure of the stack reflects the structure of the emerging parse tree. Despite this convention, we will continue to refer to the active node as the *top* of the stack.

The parser is also equipped with a *lookahead buffer* consisting of only three memory cells. Even though the precise number of cells in the buffer can only be empirically motivated, it is essential that the length of the buffer is quite limited: the Determinism Hypothesis would lose much of its interest if the parser were allowed to circumvent guesses by means of an unlimited lookahead. The buffer is the parser's *right context* and represents its data driven mode of operation. These information facilities suffice to ensure that "all sentences which people can parse without conscious difficulty can be parsed strictly deterministically" (Marcus, 1980:p.6).

2.2.3 The process structure

Before turning to a description of the actual rules that manipulate the parser's data structures, it will be helpful to have a feel for its general mode of operation. As Marcus points out,

> "[t]he parser . . . operates by attaching constituents from the buffer to the constituent at the bottom of the stack until that constituent is

> complete, at which time it is popped from the stack [and inserted in the first cell of the buffer]. If the constituents in the buffer provide clear evidence that a constituent of a given type should be initiated, a new node of that type can be created an pushed onto the stack . . ."
> (p.20)

Its operations are further restricted in that it (almost always) attaches the constituents in the buffer to higher level constituents at the bottom of the stack in left-to-right order. This is the Left-to-Right Constraint (Marcus:p.141). The Marcus parser only violates this constraint when it reestablishes the unmarked order of root clauses. Hence, such violations are transparently related to non-structure-preserving root transformations. As the parser can distinguish between root and nonroot environments, it is possible to write special purpose rules that will not be triggered in nonroot environments.

2.2.3.1 Pattern-action rules

The parser's data structures are manipulated by a grammar, which consists of so-called pattern-action rules. These rules are partially ordered by a priority scheme and are organized into rule packets[27]. The grammar interpreter only tries to match rules in active packets (i.e. packets associated with the current). A pattern is a partial description of the content of one or more buffer cells and of the two nodes in the stack that are accessible: the current node and the current cyclic node[28] (this is the first S-node in the stack). Not all nodes need appear in a rule pattern. If two rules with identical priority both match, then the rule with the most detailed pattern takes precedence. Let us consider an example of a rule packet. In (7) below three grammar rules are listed that all belong in the same rule packet, called ss-start (simple sentence start). Ss-start is the name of the rule packet that parses the initial part of matrix clauses:

[27] As Marcus points out the packeting mechanism is redundant (p.64-66). In Berwick and Weinberg's modified Marcus parser a simple X-bar driver replaces the packeting system. For details of the X-bar driver, see Berwick (1982).

[28] The motivation for the accessibility of the current cyclic will be discussed in detail later on. Note that allowing the current cyclic to be accessed by parsing rules means that the stack is not a proper first-in-first-out device.

(7) {RULE MAJOR-DECL-S in SS-START
[=np][=vp] →
Label c s,decl,major.
Deactivate ss-start. Activate parse-subj.}

{RULE YES-NO-Q in SS-START
[=auxverb][=np] →
Label c s,quest,ynquest,major.
Deactivate ss-start.Activate parse-subj.}

{RULE IMPERATIVE in SS-START
[=tnsless] →
Label c s,imper,major.
Insert the word *you* into the buffer.
Deactivate ss-start. Activate parse-subj.}

First, observe that these three rules are not ordered by priority. The reason for this is that the three rules all have different rule patterns, so that none of them can be triggered simultaneously. Rule patterns appear in these rules as a sequence of feature bundles enclosed in square brackets. Each feature bundle gives the content of one of the cells that are accessible to parsing rules (the three buffer cells, the current and the current cyclic). Note again that a pattern need not specify the content of all of these cells. A pattern is followed by a number of actions, which are listed after the arrow. These actions are executed if the preceding pattern matches and has first priority.

2.2.3.2 The primitive actions

The Marcus parser can perform a limited number of primitive actions:

(i) If there is unambiguous evidence for the existence of a particular category, a new parse node may be pushed onto the stack. This action is called "create".

(ii) The parser can remove a node in the first cell of the buffer and add it to the list of daughters of the current. This is called "attach".

(iii) The parser can remove a complete node from the stack ("pop") and insert it in the first cell of the buffer ("drop").

(iv) The parser can assign features to the current or the current cyclic. This action is called "label".

(v) The parser can associate the current with one or more rule packets. These packets contain the rules that will build the node with which they are associated. The syntax of this action is "activate <packetname>". The parser can also deassociate the current with a rule packet. The syntax of this action is "deactivate <packetname>".

(vi) The parser can "insert" a designated lexical item into a particular buffer cell.

2.2.3.3 *Three types of rules*

A close inspection of the parser's grammar rules soon reveals that the lookahead property covers three different types of lookahead strategies, each of which is associated with a different rule type.

First of all, there are Normal Rules, which inspect the buffer to guide attach-decisions (X must be attached as a daughter of Y) and labeling decisions (which in turn affect later attach-decisions). An example of this rule type is (8) below:

```
(8)   {RULE UNMARKED-ORDER IN PARSE-SUBJ
      [=np] [=verb] →
      Attach 1st to c as np.
      Deactivate parse-subj.
      Activate parse-aux.}
```

The name of the rule should be read as "rule unmarked order in the packet parse-subject". Here and in all rules that follow *c* will be used as shorthand for *the current node*. The packet *parse-subj* is associated with an S-node. The rule in (8), which is in this packet attaches a complete subject NP as the daughter of S, after which it deactivates itself and activates a packet called *parse-aux*, which does exactly what its name says it does.

Second, the parser uses Diagnostic Rules to resolve lexical ambiguities. Consider (9) below:

```
(9)   {RULE HAVE-DIAG PRIORITY:5 IN SS-START
      [=*have, tnsless] [=np] [t] →
      %If can't prove it's not a yes-no-q then assume it is.%
      If 2nd is ns, n3p or 3rd is not verb or 3rd is tnsless
      then run imperative next
      else run yes-no-q next.}
```

Let us first go through all the gibberish in this rule. Expressions like *2nd* and *3rd* are shorthand for *the second cell of the buffer* and *the third cell of the buffer*, respectively. *ns* stands for *noun singular* and *n3p* for *noun 3rd person.*

The *t* in the rule pattern is a dummy feature that always matches. This diagnostic rule tests the contents of the buffer to see whether it should run the rule that parses imperatives or the rule that parses yes/no-questions. The way it goes about this is explained in the comment, which is the bit of text between the percentage signs: it tries to prove that the sentence is an imperative, and if it does not succeed in doing so, it assumes that it is a yes/no-question. The use of *run* instead of *activate* indicates that the diagnostic rule, the rule imperative and the rule yes/no-question are all in the same packet.

Finally, the grammar includes so-called Attention Shifting Rules. These rules are always active and analyze several types of constituents as soon as their leading edge enters the buffer. As a result of this, other rules in the grammar consider the constituents made by AS-rules primitives. It is essential that all items that can begin a constituent that must be built by an AS-rule are marked as such in the parser's lexicon, because the AS-rules parse constituents in a purely bottom-up fashion. Limiting our attention to the AS-rule which builds NPs, suppose that a determiner has entered the buffer and is currently in the third cell. This will trigger AS-rule (10) below (the one-node pattern of an AS-rule is matched against all three buffer cells in the buffer and succeeds if an item in the buffer has the feature <=npstart>):

```
(10)   {AS RULE STARTNP IN CPOOL
       [=npstart] →
       Create a new np node.
       If 1st is det then activate parse-det
       else activate parse-qp-1.
       Activate npool.}
```

Cpool is the name of a clause-level packet that contains several rules that must always be active during the entire parsing process. Most of the packetnames in this rule speak for themselves, except perhaps npool, which must always be active whenever an NP is being parsed. AS-rules have the special property that they cause the grammar interpreter to shift the parser's "attention" from the actual buffer start to some later buffer cell (the third in this case) which becomes the first cell of a virtual buffer of three cells. Once the NP has been built, the buffer returns to its original state. During the attention shift all rules will see the virtual buffer start as the beginning of the buffer. Needless to say, the AS-strategy entails that the actual length of the buffer during an attention shift is no longer limited to three cells. Marcus assumes that the actual buffer length can be limited to five cells. The resulting mechanism is best viewed as a window of three cells sliding in a buffer of five.

The motivation for AS-rules is twofold. First, the runtime grammar can be considerably simplified if clause-level rules can treat NPs as primitives. Second, it can be shown that the Marcus parser must be allowed to employ *k* fully reduced lookahead symbols if it is to model human performance. Consider once again the examples in (2), repeated below:

(2) (i) Have the students who missed the exam take the makeup today.
(ii) Have the students who missed the exam taken the makeup today?

If the Marcus parser used only terminal lookahead symbols, then it would need a lookahead buffer of arbitrary length to parse these sentences. Notice that since these sentences do not give rise to a garden path effect, we clearly want the Marcus parser to analyze them without any trouble. The lookahead scheme with attention shifts yields exactly the desired effect, because it allows the parser to resolve a local ambiguity by parsing ahead a segment of the input that can be reduced to a fully reduced right context of length *k*, the size of the lookahead buffer.

2.2.4 An example parse

This section will trace the construction of a parse tree for the sentence *John has scheduled the meeting*. In order to keep the example manageable, we will not go into the details of AS-rules and assume that NPs enter the buffer fully analyzed. This example is an adapted version from an example by Marcus (pp.74-88)[29].

By convention the parser begins every parse by calling the rule initial-rule, which creates an S node and activates two packets: cpool, which contains AS-rules that are always active at the clause level, and ss-start (simple sentence-start), which contains rules that decide on the type of simple sentences. After these rules have applied, the parser is in the state depicted in (11)[30]:

---

[29]Even though I have not indicated this, I quote freely from Marcus' text in this section.

[30]In an actual parser all nodes must be given a mnemonic name (e.g. some number), so that nodes of the same category can be distinguished by their name. In this book we will not follow this practice, in order to keep representations as simple as possible.

(11) *Active Node Stack (1 deep)*
1 S/(CPOOL SS-START)

Buffer

Here the buffer is still empty. Constituents only enter the buffer on demand during the pattern matching process. As a general book-keeping procedure, we will number successive nodes in the buffer and in the stack. The packet cpool, which contains clause-level AS-rules, will not concern us here.

(12) {RULE MAJOR-DECL-S in SS-START
[=np][=verb] →
Label c s,decl,major.
Deactivate ss-start. Activate parse-subj.}

{RULE YES-NO-Q in SS-START
[=auxverb][=np] →
Label c s,quest,ynquest,major.
Deactivate ss-start.Activate parse-subj.}

{RULE IMPERATIVE in SS-START
[=tnsless] →
Label c s,imper,major.
Insert the word *you* into the buffer.
Deactivate ss-start. Activate parse-subj.}

The rules in (12) are all in the packet ss-start. The first of these, rule major-decl-s now executes with the result below:

(13) *Active Node Stack*
1 S(DECL MAJOR S)/(CPOOL PARSE-SUBJ)

Buffer
1 NP(NAME NS NSP):(John)
2 HAVE(VERB AUXVERB PRES V3S):(has)

Yet unseen words: scheduled a meeting.

The S-node has been labeled with the features <declarative> and <major S> (Marcus's term for root S), and the packet parse-subj has been activated. Thus, the S-node is now associated with two packets. Observe also that words enter the buffer fully analyzed. So, for instance, *has* has the features <verb>, <auxiliary verb>, <present tense>, <verb 3rd person singular>. It is not essential that the reader understands all of Marcus's shorthand notation. Explanations will be given where it is necessary.

The active packet parse-subj contains the rules unmarked-order and aux-inversion. The first of these matches and is executed. We give the rule in (14), and (15) shows its effect:

(14) {RULE UNMARKED-ORDER in PARSE-SUBJ
[=np][=verb] →
Attach 1st to c as np.
Deactivate parse-subj.
Activate parse-aux.}

(15) *Active Node Stack*
1 S(DECL MAJOR S)/(PARSE-AUX CPOOL)
NP:(John)

Buffer
1 HAVE(VERB AUXVERB PRES V3S):(has)

Yet unseen words: scheduled a meeting.

The NP *John* has now been attached to the S-node. We represent this by showing the NP somewhat shifted to the right. Also note that it does not have a number in front of it, because it is no longer an active (i.e. incomplete) node in the stack. Parse-aux, which analyzes all kinds of auxiliaries, is now active and after it has executed it activates parse-vp, a packet that contains the rule mvb (Main VerB). This rule creates a VP-node and attaches the main verb as its daughter. For brevity's sake, we skip parse-aux. The rule mvb and the state the parser is in after mvb has executed are given below:

(16) {RULE MVB in PARSE-VP
[=verb] →
Deactivate parse-vp.
If c is major then activate ss-final else
If c is sec then activate emb-s-final.
Attach new vp-node to c as vp.
Attach 1st to c %which is now the vp% as verb.
Activate subj-verb,cpool.}

(17) *Active Node Stack*
2 S(DECL MAJOR S)/(SS-FINAL CPOOL)
NP:(John)
AUX:(has)
VP:>>>>>
1 VP/(SUBJ-VERB CPOOL)
VERB:(scheduled)

Buffer
1 A(NPSTART DET NS N3P ...):(a)

Yet unseen words: meeting

The packet ss-final contains rules that attach final PPs (and the like) to simple sentences. Emb-s-final is similar, except that it contains rules that must decide whether a given PP must be attached to an embedded clause currently under construction or to some higher level constituent. Rule mvb contains the complex action "attach new vp-node to c as vp". This is a complex action, because it really consists of two composite actions: create and attach. The effect of the rule is to create a new VP-node, to attach it to the current and to push it onto the stack as the new current. We will use the VP:>>>>>-notation to indicate that the current has been attached to the node directly below it.

Marcus (personal communication) admits to some uncertainty as to the desirability of this complex action. Given the parser's primitive actions, he could have chosen to formulate the rule mvb like all other rules. In that case the VP would first be created and pushed onto the stack. Once completed, it would be popped from the stack and dropped into the first buffer cell, after which it would be attached to the (new) current. According to Marcus, there were no good reasons for doing things one way or the other, except, maybe, theory internal ones. As he points out, the minimal machine clearly creates first and then attaches later. We will return to this matter later on.

The packet now active is subj-verb. It consists of a set of rules that activate the appropriate packets to parse the objects and complements of a clause. In this case this results in the activation of ss-vp:

(18) {RULE OBJECTS in SS-VP
[=np] →
Attach 1st to c as np.}

{RULE VP-DONE PRIORITY:20 in SS-VP
[t] →
pop c.}

{RULE PP-UNDER-VP-1 in SS-VP
[=pp] →
If 1st fits a pp slot of the cf of c
then attach 1st to c as pp
else run vp-done next.}

The more detailed rule pattern of the first rule gets priority over the dummy pattern in the second rule and therefore this rule is executed rather than the second. The NP *a meeting*, which has been built by an AS-rule is now attached to the VP. The second rule in the packet matches next. It pops the VP from the stack. As this node has already been attached, it cannot be dropped in the buffer. The only item left in the buffer is FINALPUNC PUNC, the end of input marker. After this marker has been read and attached to the current S, the parser enters the accept state in (19):

(19) *Active Node Stack*
1 S(DECL MAJOR S)/(SS-FINAL CPOOL)
NP:(John)
AUX:(has)
VP:(scheduled a meeting)
FINALPUNC PUNC:(.)

Buffer

Yet unseen words: (none)

2.3 Some apparent counterexamples to lookahead

Weinberg (1988) discusses a so-called minimal commitment theory of parsing, first proposed by Marcus et al. (1983), which is (a model of) a strictly deterministic parser of the Marcus family of parsers that does not use lookahead. Its most important property is that it does not build a syntactic tree directly, but instead builds a description of a (set of) syntactic tree(s). Weinberg argues that a model without lookahead is psycholinguistically more plausible.

Our primary aim here is to show that Weinberg's arguments against lookahead are not very convincing. The main thrust of the counterarguments will be that, contrary to what is assumed in Weinberg (1988) and Berwick and Weinberg (1985a), the fact that the Marcus parser does not consult its lookahead before each and every step it takes is not an ad hoc property of the model. We argue that the parser's buffer strategy must be understood in terms of a more sophisticated theory about what determines the parser's locus of attention. In particular, semantic biasing should be one of the elements of such a theory. The issue of semantic biasing is a thorny one, especially if not carefully treated. The sort of biasing we will discuss is fully consistent with the autonomy thesis. In particular, we argue that no syntactic-semantic interaction ever occurs to guide attachment decisions. The only interactions that do occur have the effect that upon encountering a local ambiguity the parser forgoes its lookahead option and blindly takes a semantically biased option *that its syntactic rule base allows it to take*. This will lead to garden path effects if the semantically biased option results in a rule failure later on in the parse. We claim that the observed garden path effects remain unexplained under a minimal commitment theory.

It will be helpful if the reader has at least a vague idea of how a minimal commitment parser works. We will therefore go through a quick review of a proposal by Berwick and Weinberg (1985a) and of the general approach to deterministic parsing of which this proposal is an instance.

2.3.1 Parsing with assertion sets

Berwick and Weinberg (1985a) propose a variant of the Marcus model which is deterministic in the following sense:

> At any step i in a parse we denote the representation of the sentence analysis at that point by A_i. A parse will be said to be deterministic if and only if the sequence of sets A_1, A_2, ..., is monotonically increasing in an information theoretic sense: each set in the sequence is either the same as or is a refinement of its predecessor."
> (p.16)

The crucial difference between this (1985a) model and that in Berwick and Weinberg (1984) is that, whereas the latter built explicit tree structure, this new parser builds as its output a set representing all and only the *is-a* and *left-to-right precedence* relations in a sentence. Intermediate sets may be underspecified, subject to refinement as evidence about the structure of the input sentence accumulates with every new input item. Assuming that the positions between the words in the input are numbered, the phrase marker may be represented as a set of triples, each consisting of a phrasal name, and its start position and its stop position. Assertion set parsers implement a wait-and-see strategy that is quite different from a wait-and-see strategy using lookahead.

Marcus (1987) gives the following exegesis on Description Theory (Marcus et al. 1983), which is another name for minimal commitment theory:

> "The philosophy underlying [Description Theory] is that a sentence is a physical entity, an acoustic entity, in much the same sense that this chair in front of me is a physical entity. And a parse of a sentence has to be viewed as a description of that sentence in the same way that my visual faculty parses the scene including this chair. So after I recognize the chair [a moulded fiberglass chair, in this case] as an entity, as part of recognizing that it's a chair, presumably, I break it up into having two arms, a back and a seat, even though of course the distinction between the arms and the back is just virtual. I derive a functional description of this thing, a functional description of an object which in some real sense isn't there in the world at all *per se*. Similarly, one parses a sonic utterance up into words, even though the words aren't physically distinct, and then the phrase structure analyzer in your head describes that putative word string at this somewhat higher level of functional detail. The key point is that syntactic structures aren't entities in my head; what I have in my head is a description of a syntactic structure which is imputed to be out there in the world." (pp.83-84)

We see then that assertion set parsing involves a very important conceptual shift. Berwick and Weinberg's assertion set parser is a parser of the D-theory family that does not use lookahead. As can be shown with a very simple example, a deterministic parser without lookahead cannot use an explicit rewrite rule approach. Consider (20) (examples from Berwick and Weinberg):

(20) (i) 0 I 1 know 2 that 3 block 4 supports 5 the 6 pyramid 7
(ii) 0 I 1 know 2 that 3 blocks 4 support 5 the 6 pyramid 7

The point is that if the parser can only use literals such as complementizer and NP, then the parser will have to retract many of its decisions. In (20) above for example, *that* is locally ambiguous: it could either be a determiner or a complementizer. Without lookahead the parser will evidently be wrong some of the time. For that reason, the authors propose to incorporate the X'-theory directly in the parser, and to allow it to underspecify a head's categorial features. In addition, it is assumed that a verb such as *know* subcategorizes for some XP, and that all heads project onto the phrasal level. In the examples that follow we also assume, following the version of X'-theory in Chomsky (1986), that INFL and COMP project like any other category. Hence, we assume that INFL (henceforth: I) projects to IP (=S) and that specIP is the position of the structural subject. COMP (henceforth: C) projects to CP (=S'), complementizers appear at the head of CP, while *wh*-movement is to specCP. The basic clausal skeleton has the form below:

```
           CP
          /  \
     SPEC     C'
             /  \
            C    IP
                /  \
            SPEC    I'
                   /  \
                  I    VP
                      /  \
                    ...  ...
```

Let us review Berwick and Weinberg's sketch of the analysis of the examples above, beginning with (20i). When the parser sees *that*, it has already built up the assertion set below:

(21) (I,0,1) (NP,0,1)
(know,1,2) (VP,1,*)
(XP,2,*)

The last triple has been added because *know* predicts that an XP starts after it. When the parser has read *that*, we have the assertion set (22):

(22) (I,0,1) (NP,0,1)
(know,1,2) (VP,1,*)
(XP,2,*)
(that,2,3) (XP,2,*)

We now have two identical triples (XP,2,*). The first is predicted by *know*, and the second is the maximal projection of *that* (which is as yet underdetermined). After *block*, we can refine the last of these triples:

(23) (I,0,1) (NP,0,1)
(know,1,2) (VP,1,*)
(XP,2,*)
(that,2,3) (DETP,2,3)
(block,3,4) (NP,2,*)

When the parser finally sees *support*, it adds compatible assertions and refines the first XP to a CP:

(24) (I,0,1) (NP,0,1)
(know,1,2) (VP,1,*)
(CP,2,*)
(that,2,3) (DETP,2,3)
(block,3,4) (NP,2,4)
(supports,4,5) (VP,4,*)

When all input has been read, we have the assertion set below:

(25) (I,0,1) (NP,0,1)
(know,1,2) (VP,1,7)
(CP,2,7)
(that,2,3) (DETP,2,3)
(block,3,4) (NP,2,4)
(supports,4,5) (VP,4,7)
(the,5,6) (DETP,5,6)
(pyramid,6,7) (NP,5,7)

In the case of (20ii), the parser again predicts an XP after *know*, and asserts an underspecified projection for *that*, as in (22) above. Now the parser sees *blocks*, a plural noun:

> "Based on this information, it can now refine the X-max triple to [CP]. We also add the new projection [(NP,3,*)] (for the NP headed by *blocks*), and one for an [IP]; note that this is aways allowed. Eventually the [CP] will stretch from position 2 through 7; the IP from 3 through 7."
> (p.22)

The final assertion set has the form below:

(26) (I,0,1) (NP,0,1)
(know,1,2) (VP,1,7)
(CP,2,7)
(that,2,3) (CP,2,7)
(IP,3,7)
(blocks,3,4) (NP,3,4)
(support,4,5) (VP,4,7)
(the,5,6) (DETP,5,6)
(pyramid,6,7) (NP,5,7)

This concludes our example.

According to Berwick and Weinberg assertion set parsing has the following advantages over the old Marcus model:

- Because of the underspecification method, the system does not make any decisions it has to retract. This will also be true of ambiguous sentences[31]. They mention the example of PP-attachment ambiguity: in that case none of the possibilities will be asserted.
- Assertion sets can be filtered via any predicate whatsoever, which makes it easy to fold in the effects of lexical preferences, or whatever one wants.
- Because no look-ahead is ever used, short garden paths, such as *the boat floated sank* are at least possible; Parsifal has to deliberately ignore its own look-ahead in an ad hoc way in order to garden path in such cases.

With this background we now discuss a number of constructions that have been claimed are incompatible with the assumption of lookahead.

2.3.2 Some constructions claimed to be incompatible with lookahead

2.3.2.1 Lookahead and the structure of NPs

The first problem in connection with lookahead that Weinberg (1988) discusses is that "we must either make the lookahead buffer so capacious as to be psycholinguistically implausible, or incorrectly predict that certain sentences that are in fact quite easy to process will cause the processor to make mistakes". She gives (27) as an example of the sort of sentences that make the point:

(27) I drove my aunt from a small town in Wisconsin's car into the city

Her argument runs as follows. When the parser has started to build the VP initiated by *drove*, the buffer contains the words *my* to *town* (assuming a buffer of 5 cells). Therefore, the most the parser can assume is that it has seen the complex NP *my aunt from a small town.* If the parser attaches this NP, then it incorrectly predicts that the NP functions as the direct object of *drove.* Weinberg implicitly assumes that this would be a bad result, a matter to which we return directly below. She then goes on to argue against Marcus (1980) solution to this problem. Parsifal would build the complex NP *my aunt from a small town in Wisconsin* using the AS-strategy, before deciding where to attach it in the tree, as required. According to Weinberg, this would commit the parser to storing large amounts of material whose logical role is unknown, which "should quickly overburden short term memory" (cf. Miller 1951). She concludes that "we would

---

[31]The original Marcus parser could have been designed to output all and only the correct structures *without underspecification.* So the advantage claimed here is somewhat dubious.

incorrectly predict that sentences with constituents of this type should be difficult to understand".

Weinberg's criticism is misguided for a number of reasons. To begin with, sentences like (27) above *are* difficult, contrary to what she suggests. What is more, sentence (27) is close to unacceptable under the intended reading. It certainly is not "quite easy to process" [sic!]. The only readings that informants agree are truly easy to get are given in (28i,ii):

(28) (i) I drove [my aunt from a small town] [in Wisconsin's car] [into the city]
(ii) I drove [my aunt] [from a small town] [in Wisconsin's car] [into the city]

Second, Marcus approach avoids overburdening of short term memory rather than giving rise to it. Parsifal builds the entire specifier and drops it in the buffer after completion. Hence, the only node in the buffer whose logical role is unknown is the NP-node itself. All elements *inside* the NP have already been analyzed. In fact, this is an example of Parsifal's standard treatment of completed phrases: there is nothing exceptional about dropping completed phrases in the first cell of the buffer.

Third, consider what would be predicted under a minimal commitment theory. At each step in a parse a minimal commitment parser adds all assertions that are compatible with the input it has seen. Whatever it does not know for sure it need not assert. Because (27) is globally ambiguous, a minimal commitment model must underspecify the syntactic structure, so that its output is compatible with all possible readings. It therefore does not distinguish between easy and difficult readings for (27). It is not even clear what will keep such a parser from effortlessly analyzing sentences like (29):

(29) I drove my mother from a big town in Holland's aunt from a small town in Wisconsin's grandmother from an unknown village in Alaska's snowsled into New York

Finally, note that the underspecification technique may in some cases produce outputs that are quite severely underspecified. This raises the question when and how the syntactic structure of particular readings of multiply ambiguous strings is to be recovered.

2.3.2.2 Frazier and Rayner's (1982) reading experiment

Weinberg (1988) discusses a reading experiment conducted by Frazier and Rayner (1982), in which subjects were asked to read a variety of locally ambiguous sentences. The experiment measured subjects' eye movements. Some sample data are given below (from Weinberg 1988):

(30) (i) Mary expected Fred
     (ii) Mary expected Fred to arrive
(31) (i) The lawyers think that his second wife will claim the inheritance
     (ii) His second wife will claim the inheritance belongs to her
(32) (i) Since Jay always jogs a mile this seems like a very short distance to him
     (ii) Since Jay always jogs a mile seems like a very short distance to him

These sentences were presented without a disambiguating comma. The result of the experiment was that the (ii) sentences were more difficult to process than the (i) sentences. The eye movement measurements revealed that subjects spent a long period of time gazing at the disambiguating part of sentences (e.g. *belongs* in (31ii)) and they also showed regressive eye movements to the point of local ambiguity (e.g. *the inheritance* in (31ii)). Frazier and Rayner claim that this pattern is incompatible with parallel processing, because such a model would simply discard the wrong analysis at the point of disambiguation, which would neither explain the gaze duration at the disambiguating material nor the regressive eye movements.

Weinberg points out that things look just as bad for a deterministic device with lookahead:

> "Given that a deterministic device of the Marcus (1980) variety cannot misparse any material, we would expect it to pause at a locally ambiguous segment [in both the (i) and (ii) sentences] because it must look ahead in order to unambiguously decide how to proceed. However, longer gaze duration was not observed at the ambiguous position in any of the sentences. We would also expect regressive eye movements following lookahead in *both cases*.
>
> By contrast, if we assume that a backtracking parser always pursues one analysis preferentially, then we expect the observed asymmetries."
>
> (pp.46-47)

She then goes on to argue that the results of this experiment are fully compatible with a minimal commitment parser. As we will not debate this final conclusion, the reader is referred to Weinberg (1988) for particulars. Here we will give arguments that Weinberg's conclusion that the results of this experiment are inconsistent with a parser with lookahead is unwarranted.

First, observe that there is a world of difference between a sentence like (30ii) and a sentence like (32ii). Both are repeated directly below for convenience:

(30) (ii) Mary expected Fred to arrive
(32) (ii) Since Jay always jogs a mile seems like a very short distance to him

Sentence (32ii) elicits a strong garden path in most people, whereas (30ii) presents no noticeable difficulties. Interestingly, a parser with lookahead can account for the observed contrast, if we take the standard view that the way in which a parser uses its lookahead is totally dependent on its rule base. Upon reading *expect* in (30ii), the parser consults its lexicon and finds that *expect* is associated with three subcategorization frames: it expects to see an NP, an IP or a CP next. It is therefore driven to look ahead *beyond* the NP in the first buffer cell so as to decide what to do next. Now consider what happens in (32ii). When the parser encounters *jog*, its lexicon informs it that *jog* is either intransitive or followed by an NP-object. Therefore, the parser consults the first buffer cell to see if the buffer contains an NP. Because it does, this NP is attached as a sister to the verb *jog*. This eventually leads to disaster, because the parser is led down the garden path. What we are saying then, is that the parser is a very limited and even stupid machine that cannot "remember" that it is parsing an adjunct. It simply acts upon the expectations sparked by the elements in its input.

Second, both Frazier and Rayner's and Weinberg's interpretation of the experimental results suppresses a very prominent aspect of the experimental material: the effect of semantic biases. Consider the following pairs:

(33) (i) His second wife will claim the inheritance belongs to her
(ii) His second wife will believe the inheritance belongs to her
(34) (i) Since Jay always jogs a mile seems like a very short distance to him
(ii) Since Jay always jogs running shoes seem like normal footwear to him

Most people seem to be led down the garden path in the (i) cases, whereas the (ii) cases present no noticeable difficulties. Given what we have said so far, the observed garden path effect in (33i) is unexpected. After having analyzed *claim*, the parser expects to see an NP or CP next. Hence, one would expect it to look ahead beyond the NP in the first buffer cell, which predicts the absence of a garden path effect. Now observe that this is exactly what we find in the structurally parallel case (33ii). This strongly suggests that the garden path effect in (33i) is due to a semantic bias: semantically speaking, the NP following *claim* is such a likely candidate for an NP object that the parser seems to forgo the option to look ahead any further.

Let us briefly step back and consider the implications of our suggestion for the theory of online sentence processing. For the syntactic parser to be sensitive to semantic cues it must be the case that the semantic interpretation of the input sentence is built alongside the syntactic representation and that semantic expectations are fed back into the syntactic parser. Notice that this does not commit us to the claim that syntactic processing is not autonomous. We could and will maintain that even though semantic feedback may affect syntactic parsing decisions, semantic feedback never takes precedence over syntactic rules. Our suggestion amounts to the claim that semantic feedback may, for better or for worse, decrease the syntactic parser's search space in certain cases[32], thus speeding up syntactic processing at the cost of occasional errors[33].

Returning now to our discussion of the sentences above, observe that in (33ii), by contrast, there is a strong semantic bias against taking the NP to be the object. In this case it is very hard to determine whether the parser makes use of its ability to look ahead beyond the material following the NP at all. In particular, it is difficult to determine whether a sentence like (35) is just semantically strange or whether it is garden path as well:

(35) His second wife will believe the inheritance

In (34ii) the parser consults the first buffer cell, as it clearly must to determine if there is an NP in the buffer, but the NP it finds is such an unlikely direct object from a semantic point of view that it assumes the intransitive reading of *jog*. Just in case the reader does not feel quite sure that this is what happens:

[32]Although the notion of search space is normally associated with nondeterminism, I use it here to refer to the parser's inspection of the contents of the buffer.

[33]See Jackendoff (1987) for a discussion of models of sentence processing along the lines briefly sketched here.

(36) Since Jay always jogs running shoes a mile seems like a short distance to him

This sentence is not just semantically anomolous: it produces a very strong garden path. If the parser does not look ahead beyond the first NP, this is precisely what one would expect. If, on the other hand, the parser did look ahead beyond the NP *running shoes*, one would be at pains to account for the observed garden path effect.

We conclude that the Frazier and Rayner experiment does not force us to give up the idea of lookahead. Instead, the results suggest that we develop a more sophisticated theory of what determines the way in which the parser uses its lookahead buffer. It may be tentatively concluded that the selectional properties of analyzed material impose a strict bound on the number of buffer cells that the parser ever inspects and that the extent to which the parser makes use of its lookahead is also subject to semantic biasing.

At least part of the asymmetries in (33) and (34) remain unaccounted for under a minimal commitment theory. In particular, it is unclear how a minimal commitment parser could ever be truly led down the garden path in a sentence like (34ii). The point is that such a model need not commit itself to one of the alternative analyses. It will therefore not be led down the garden path in (34ii). This predicts that (37i) and (37ii) are equally (un)problematic, which is clearly incorrect:

(37) (i) Mary expected Fred to arrive
(ii) Since Jay always jogs a mile seems like a short distance to him

2.3.2.3 Short garden paths

Following several other researchers[34], Weinberg (1988) argues that a parser with even minimal lookahead should be able to process short garden paths like (38):

(38) [$_{IP}$ [$_{NP}$the boat floated] sank]

The reasoning behind this criticism of the lookahead buffer seems straightforward: because the parser can see the second verbal element in the buffer, it "knows" that it should create a relative clause. Berwick and Weinberg (1985a) say about this: "The Marcus parser had to deliberately ignore its own

[34] See for instance Fodor (1985) and Berwick and Weinberg (1985a).

lookahead information in an ad hoc way in order to garden path in such cases" (p.23).

This criticism of the lookahead buffer is rather unenlighting, however. The key fact about garden paths is not that Parsifal's buffer strategy does not account for the short ones, but that it fails to account for most of the long ones as well. Consider the following contrast:

(39) (i) the horse raced past the barn fell
(ii) the car expected to drive badly won the race

Most people seem to agree that (39i) leads one down the garden path when one reads it for the first time. No such effect occurs in (39ii), even though, as in (39i), the disambiguating information is outside the parser's lookahead. And, of course, exactly the same contrast can be found with shorter sentences:

(40) (i) the boat floated sank
(ii) the boat painted sank

Again we see that the parser can be fooled by what we have called semantic biases. The garden path facts are explained if we assume that the selectional frame of the verb being analyzed is the pivot on which the parser's buffer strategy turns. If the NP preceding the verb has the right semantics for the verb's external θ-role, then the parser looks no further and analyzes the NP as the verb's subject. If, on the other hand, the semantics of the NP is incompatible with the external θ-role, then the parser blindly embarks upon the relative clause analysis. The following "inverted" garden path[35] again suggests that the relative clause is initiated without looking ahead beyond the verb:

(41) the boat painted

Notice that only the short garden paths can give us a clue about this, because in the case of a long inverted garden path, looking ahead would not help anyway (assuming a buffer of three cells):

(42) the car expected to drive badly

[35]"Inverted" because one mistakenly assumes the relative clause analysis and not the no relative clause analysis, as with standard examples of garden paths.

The results of this analysis confirm the hypothesis that the lookahead strategy is never used to scan material independently of the selectional properties of heads. In addition we have adduced arguments that lookahead is sometimes forgone in the face of strong semantic biases.

2.4 Some suggestions for a theory of the buffer

In the foregoing discussion we have made a number of suggestions concerning the buffer mechanism. We will summarize these ideas below.

The Marcus parser is assumed to have three buffer cells (i.e. a lookahead of two cells). However, the actual number of buffer cells is partly a function of the parser's rule base. For instance, the length of the buffer is increased in case an Attention Shifting rule executes. Apart from that, it can be argued on quite simple grounds that a buffer of three cells is insufficient for a language like Dutch. Consider, for instance, such cases as in (43) below:

(43) (i) . . . dat Jan Cruyff Tigana een trap zag verkopen
. . . that John Cruyff Tigana a kick saw sell
. . . that John saw Cruyff give Tigana a kick
(ii) . . . dat Jan Marie Piet een verklaring schuldig acht
. . . that John Mary Pete an explanation owing considered
. . . that John considered Mary to owe Pete an explanation

Even if we assume that in each of these sentences *Jan* can be identified as the subject and therefore attached to the current, we still need a buffer of at least four cells if the parser is to see the first verb. Once we assume a four-cell buffer for Dutch, it seems reasonable to assume a four-cell buffer four English as well. This has the consequence that the length of the buffer can no longer be used to account for garden paths. Because this account was not satisfactory anyway, we need not worry too much about that.

The existence of AS-rules on the one hand and the view of lookahead that we have developed in the previous sections suggest a rather different approach to the buffer mechanism. Suppose the buffer is really short term memory, as has been suggested by several researchers (including Marcus himself), then we might expect it to have a *physical* length of seven plus or minus two cells. We have some evidence that in actual use only part of this buffer is ever consulted by grammar rules[36]. Perhaps the *apparent* length of the buffer (somewhere between 3 to 6 cells) can be explained as an epiphenomenon of the parser's acquisition procedure. In a head-initial language like English, rule generalization will presumably have the effect that most of the time only one or two buffer cells will need to be specified in a rule pattern. This would presumably work out rather differently for head-final languages, especially if we were to assume, as we will do in chapter 3, that the parser's decision to attach a completed phrase is dependent upon the presence of a selecting head. Since these suggestions uncover enough questions to prompt a new research proposal[37], we will not go into any further details.

2.5 Berwick and Weinberg's modified Marcus parser

Berwick and Weinberg's (1984) investigation is based on a modified version of the Marcus parser, which implements the Government Binding Theory (Chomsky 1981). Although the authors do not specify an explicit rule component, we may assume that the parser they have in mind is the modified version of Parsifal described in Berwick (1982,1985). Berwick's new parser design eliminates the original packet control of rules and instead uses an X'-control that subsumes the *create node* and *drop node* grammar rule actions. None of these changes affects the basic properties of the Marcus parser and for our purposes we may assume that Berwick and Weinberg's modified Marcus parser and Parsifal are basically the same.

There is one respect in which the new parser design is an extension of the basic Marcus design. Berwick and Weinberg's model consists of two parsers, whose operations are "pipelined", so that the second can read the output of the first. The first stage of this cascade of parsers is a strictly deterministic Marcus type machine that outputs just one derivation for every input. Its rules are stored in a finite control table and stated in terms of actual grammar symbols: no variables are allowed in this table. Berwick (1982,1985) and Berwick &

---

[36]It might be interesting to investigate how much of the buffer is used by other rule systems. It seems quite reasonable to assume that the buffer is a work space for syntactic, phonological, morphological and semantic rules alike. There are several facts that point in this direction. We have mentioned semantic biasing. Marcus et al. (1983) suggest that phonological rules use the buffer for creating intonational phrases. It is rather uncontroversial to assume that morphological rules operate upon the contents of the buffer as well.

[37]Consider, for instance, the problem posed by rule generalization. When does the parser's (hypothetical) acquisition procedure have evidence that a particular rule may be generalized? On the assumption that the procedure does not have access to negative data, no such evidence would ever seem to be available.

Weinberg (1984) claim that this parser can be modeled by a restricted kind of LR(k) parser called a Bounded Context Parser (this is actually incorrect, but see the following section). Such machines perform in time O(n) (read *of order n*), where n measures the "size" of the problem (i.e. the size of the input, conceived of as a string of symbols). Therefore, this type of parser may be regarded as extremely efficient. The second stage of the parser calculates referential dependencies. With Fodor (1985), I confess to some uncertainty about the exact properties of this machine. As it consists of a search algorithm, which can, in principle at least, search an unbounded domain for an antecedent, it cannot be a Bounded Context Parser (henceforth BCP). However, Berwick and Weinberg suggest that it is a BCP after all when they say: "Our overall goal will be to show that the two stage model can be viewed as a cascade of bounded context transducers" (p.183). Their discussion of coindexing efficiency (p.193ff.) seems to indicate that the search procedure can consider all preceding NPs in a sentence, which would mean that the second stage machine cannot be bounded. Schematically, the model they describe looks like this:

(44) Two stage parser

Stage 1	Input: morph. analyzed surface sentence Bounded context (?) parser (Machine 1)
	Output: annotated S-structure (no indices)
Stage 2	Input to second stage
	Bounded context (?) parser (Machine 2) Output: annotated S-structure (with indices)

As was pointed out in 1.4.5, the relationship between Parsifal's runtime grammar and the grammatical theory that Marcus assumed is no stronger than covering equivalence. This carries over to Berwick and Weinberg's modified version. They take the view that "unlike the grammar, the parser is a device designed to perform a specific task", and that "the particular exigencies of parsing can influence implementation details" (p.143). This is quite consonant with the view expressed by Marr (1982), discussed in the previous chapter, that finding algorithms by which a grammatical theory may be implemented is a different endeavour from formulating the theory itself. While the modified Marcus parser makes direct use of the grammar in that it makes crucial reference to lexical properties of items at every level of representation in accordance with the Projection Principle (Chomsky,1981)[38], there is no one-to-one relation between rules and operations of the grammar and rules and operations of the parser. Still, the parser embeds the key principles of Government Binding Theory (e.g. X-bar theory) fairly directly.

2.6 Formal properties of the Marcus parser: LR(k), BCP(m,n), and LRRL(k) grammars

What follows below is a short and rather technical digression into some formal properties of the Marcus parser. The key results of this section will be informally reintroduced later on as the need arises.

As is shown by Nozohoor-Farshi (1986), the class of grammars parsable by a Marcus-type parser is neither a subclass of LR(k) grammars nor a subclass of BCP(m,n) grammars, but a subclass of LRRL(k) grammars.

An LR(k) parser computes a rightmost derivation in reverse, using *k* terminal lookahead symbols. A rightmost derivation goes from the fringe (the terminal symbols) to the root (the topmost S of the tree)[39] from right to left. The derivation of the string *aadbb* given below is rightmost with respect to the grammar G_i (the example grammar is from Nozohoor-Farshi 1986; the numbers above the arrows indicate rule numbers):

Grammar G_i:

(1) S'→S
(2) S→d
(3) S→A S B
(4) A→a
(5) A→a S
(6) B→b

[38]The same is true of the original Marcus parser, though implicitly so, as at that time this property was not defined in terms of the Projection Principle. It should be clear, however, that the Marcus parser derives its ability to insert argument traces from access to the selectional properties of lexical items. In fact, many other previous parsing models have implicitly assumed the existence of a similar principle as a way of detecting expected gaps in the input.

[39]I.e. LR(k) parsing is bottom-up.

$$S' \xrightarrow{1} S \xrightarrow{3} ASB \xrightarrow{6} ASb \xrightarrow{3} AASBb \xrightarrow{6} AASbb \xrightarrow{2} AAdbb$$

$$\xrightarrow{4} Aadbb \xrightarrow{4} aadbb$$

An LR(k) parser which parses the string *aadbb* with respect to G_i produces this derivation in reverse order. The parser consists of a stack, a lookahead buffer of length *k*, an output tape, and a so-called LR(k) table that acts as the parser's finite control[40]. At every step in the parse, the finite control dictates to what new state it should go and what action (either a shift or a reduce) it should perform given some input symbol, *k* lookahead symbols, and current state. If the parser has performed a reduce, the number of the corresponding production (or rewrite rule) is written on the output tape.

The Marcus parser is quite similar to an LR(k) parser in many respects. Berwick (1985) contains an informal discussion of these similarities, although no formal method is presented for converting Marcus's grammar rules together with the packeting mechanism into an LR(k) table[41]. In the Marcus parser, the packeting mechanism effectively serves as an encoding of left context. Further, instead of writing rule numbers on an output tape, the Marcus parser builds an explicit tree structure.

To show that the Marcus parser can in fact *not* be modeled by an LR(k) machine, Nozohoor-Farshi (1986) uses the example grammar G_i above. This grammar is not LR(k) for any fixed *k*. The problem is that any *a* can be reduced to an *A* via production $A \rightarrow a$ or can be considered as a first symbol in the production $A \rightarrow aS$ (i.e. a shift/reduce conflict). However, in the first case *a* is followed by an *Sb*, and in the latter by an *Sd* or an *Sa*. For any fixed lookahead of length *k*, there will always be sentences generated by this grammar with a prefix a^n, $n>k$. By contrast, G_i can be parsed by a Marcus parser, because for each *a* it can create an *A* and attach *a* as a daughter of *A*, while postponing the completion of each *A* until it reaches the disambiguating context. See Nozohoor-Farshi for a detailed explication of this result.

---

[40]The parsing algorithm for an LR(k) parser is based on the construction of a deterministic finite state automaton that is used for the recognition of possible left contexts. The information extracted from this automaton takes the form of an LR(k) table that is used as a finite state control.

[41]As we will see shortly, a Marcus parser cannot be converted into an LR(k) parser. Conversely, an LR(k) parser can be converted into a Marcus parser. See Nijenhuis (1989) for a formal proof of this result and an example of such a conversion.

Nozohoor-Farshi demonstrates that G_i is not LR(k,t) either. LR(k,t) grammars were originally proposed by Knuth (1965). LR(k,t) parsing is an extension of the basic LR(k) method. This extension is identical to LR(k) parsing, except that, instead of the leftmost phrase of a right sentential form[42], we must be able to determine that in any sentential form at least one of the *t* (a fixed number) leftmost phrases is reducible to a specific non-terminal. As Nozohoor-Farshi puts it: ". . . a grammar G is not LR(k,t) if in parsing of an input sentence the decision about reduction of *t* or more questionable [i.e. locally ambiguous-jvdk] phrases in a sentential form needs to be delayed. The reduction decision is reached by examining the whole left context and *k* symbols to the right of a phrase in a sentential form."

The demonstration that G_i is not LR(k,t) proceeds as follows:

> Now, it is easy to see that G_i is not LR(k,t) for any finite numbers k and t. For given k and t, $L(G_i)$[43] includes sentences with prefix a^n where n>k+t. In such sentences t initial *a*'s have different interpretations depending on the other parts of the sentences. For example consider the two sentences:
>
> (I) $a^n db^n$ (n>k+t) (II) $a^n(db)^n$ (n>k+t)

```
      S'                         S'
      |                          |
      S                          S
    / | \                      / | \
   A  |  B                   A   S   B
   |  |  |                 / |   |   |
   a  S  b                a  S   d   b
     /|\                   / | \
    A | B                 A  S  B
    | | |                /|  |  |
    a S b               a S  d  b
      .                   .
      .                   .
      .                   .
      S                   S
    / | \               / | \
   A  S  B             A  S  B
   |  |  |             |  |  |
   a  d  b             a  d  b
```

> In (I) all t initial *a*'s must be reduced to *A*'s, while in (II) none of

[42]A right sentential form is one of the successive lines of a rightmost derivation.

[43]The language generated by G_i.

them is a phrase. Therefore an LR(k,t) parser will need to delay reduction of more than t possible phrases in parsing of a sentence with a prefix a^n, n>k+t, and thus G_i is not LR(k,t) for any given number k and t. In fact, LR(k,t) parsers put a limit t on the number of delayed decisions at any time during the parsing. In Marcus parsing, depending on characteristics of the grammar, there may be no limit on this number."
(Nozohoor-Farshi 1986:p. 534)

Having shown that the class of Marcus parsers is not a subset of the class of LR(k,t) parsers, the author also shows that the class of LR(k,t) parsers is not a subset of the class of Marcus parsers. See Nozohoor-Farshi (1986) for a demonstration of this result.

Nozohoor-Farshi also points out that it is trivial to show that BCP grammars are unsuitable for formalizing the Marcus parser, contrary to what is claimed by Berwick (1985) and Berwick & Weinberg (1984). The point is simply that a BCP ignores information that is extractable from the left context (except for the last m symbols), whereas the Marcus parser uses the packeting mechanism exactly for this purpose. He gives the example grammar below to make his point:

Grammar G_j:
(1) $S \rightarrow aA$
(2) $S \rightarrow bB$
(3) $A \rightarrow d$
(4) $A \rightarrow cA$
(5) $B \rightarrow d$
(6) $B \rightarrow cB$

After attaching the first symbol in the input, the Marcus parser will activate different rule packets to parse *A* or *B*, depending on whether the first symbol was an *a* or a *b*. A BCP, however, cannot reduce the *d* in the sentences *ac...cd* and *bc...cd*, because a number of *c*'s greater than m shields the necessary context for reduction of *A→d* or *B→d*.

Nozohoor-Farshi concludes his paper by introducing LRRL(k) parsing. A basic LRRL(k) parser parses its input in a *L*eft-to-*R*ight manner using *k* symbols fully *R*educed *L*ookaheads. The class of Marcus parsers is a subclass of the class of LRRL(k) parsers. The author explains that the parsing algorithm for an LRRL(k) grammar is based on the construction of a Characteristic Finite State Machine (CFSM), which is quite similar to the deterministic finite state automaton that is used in LR(k) parsing for the generation of LR(k) tables.

Thus, the information extracted from the CFSM is in tabulated form that acts as the finite control for the parsing algorithm. The major characteristic that distinguishes LRRL(k) parsers from LR(k) parsers is the nature of the lookaheads: the most general class of LRRL(k) parsers considers lookaheads at arbitrary levels, whereas LR(k) parsers only use bare terminals as lookahead.

2.7 LRRL(k) parsing and functional explanation

2.7.1 Berwick and Weinberg's functional explanation of Subjacency

Following in the footsteps of Marcus, Berwick and Weinberg argue that a strictly deterministic model of the human sentence processor provides functional explanations for the existence of otherwise unexplained constraints of current transformational theories of grammar. In particular, it is claimed that a Marcus type model of parsing explains the existence of the Subjacency restriction on overt movement. Let us go through their argument step by step.

The main problem for a strictly deterministic parser is local ambiguity. As the parser can construct just one syntactic tree representation for every sentence and cannot undo previous actions, it must resolve any ambiguity it comes across before it can continue the parse.

Consider the following sentences:

(45) (i) Who_i did John kiss t_i?
(ii) $What_i$ did John say t_i that Frank believed t_i that Sue said . . . t_i that Bill would like to eat t_i?
(iii) Did John say that Frank believed that Sue said that Bill would like to eat?

Structure (45i), in particular the insertion of the postverbal trace, is unproblematic for the parser. Remember that the parser has direct access to the properties of lexical items. Hence, recognition of the verb *kiss* entails retrieval of that item's subcategorization frame as well. As *kiss* is a transitive verb, the parser will expect to see an NP next. If there is no phonological NP, then the parser will simply attach an empty NP (a trace) as the object of *kiss*, as the Projection Principle requires *kiss* to have an object. Note that strictly local information (i.e. government) precludes insertion of a PRO. Now consider (45ii). *Eat* may be either transitive or intransitive. Given strict determinism, the parser must decide what to do before it can proceed to the next item in the input stream. Clearly, the ambiguity can only be resolved by consulting the left context to see if there is an appropriate antecedent. If an appropriate antecedent is found, the parser will assume that *eat* is transitive and insert a trace. If, on the other hand, the left context does not contain an appropriate antecedent, the parser will do nothing and move on to the next item in the input stream.

As can be seen in (45ii), the site for trace insertion can be arbitrarily far away from its phonological antecedent. This means that the relevant parsing rule would have to refer to a potentially unbounded left context (assuming now that there are no intermediate traces). Such a rule could be finitely stated in terms of an essential variable, but this option is not available to the rule format of a Marcus-type parser. The reason for this is that Marcus-type parsers are a subclass of LRRL(k) parsers, which use a finite control table to guide parsing decisions. A finite control only uses literals (i.e. actual input symbols and grammatical categories), not variables. It follows that a Marcus parser can only detect an antecedent in a literally finite left context. Hence, the parser must have a trace insertion procedure for intermediate traces. It follows that the existence of a bounding condition can be explained in terms of a particular class of parsers, the LRRL(k) parsers.

It remains to be explained, however, why the bounding condition on overt movement should take the form of Subjacency:

(46) Subjacency
No rule can involve X and Y in the configuration:
$[\ldots X\ldots[_{\alpha}\ldots[_{\beta}\ldots Y\ldots]\ldots]\ldots X\ldots]$
where α and ß are bounding nodes.

Why should the limit on the number of bounding nodes be one rather than, say, ten? Berwick and Weinberg argue that the reason for this is that natural rule systems cannot express numerical values. In other words, natural grammars cannot count. There is, however, one numerical value which coincides with a structural characteristic, namely in the case of the structural characteristic *adjacency*. One might also ask why the bounding nodes are NP and S rather than AP and VP. Again the answer is that this must be specified by the grammar. Thus, Berwick and Weinberg argue, the structure of the parser together with the grammatical primitive adjacency explains the existence of Subjacency[44,45].

[44]Both Marcus and Berwick and Weinberg have been criticized on the grounds that their functional explanation of subjacency is essentially circular. See, for instance, Van de Koot (1987) and Fodor (1985). These authors begin by observing that the functional explanation of subjacency hinges on the crucial assumption that both the current node (the top node in the stack) and the current cyclic (the first S-node in the stack) are transparent for parsing rules. They then point out that, since no independent motivation is offered for the accessibility of the

2.7.2 A critical examination: LRRL(k) parsing and restricted annotation

Berwick and Weinberg's account is rather sketchy and suppresses some important properties of LRRL(k) parsing that have far-reaching consequences with respect to the functional account they present. In particular, an LRRL(k) parser can encode left context by means of feature annotation on the current, on condition that the current node is always literally finite. Berwick (1985) points out that the standard method for encoding left context in an LR(k) parser, which is a subclass of the class of LRRL(k) parsers, involves using feature annotations on all the maximal projection between the phonetic antecedent and the trace insertion site:

> ". . . since grammar rules can make reference to not only the top element of the stack, but also to the so-called *current cyclic node*, we must have some way to encode this information as well. When a new active node is formed, its current cyclic node is simply the cyclic node of the node that was just active, unless a new cyclic (NP or S) node has been formed in the meantime. In either case, we can simply code an active node as the pair (active node, cyclic node)".
> (1985:pp.316-317)

We see, then, that an LRRL(k) parser can encode the presence of an antecedent that may be indefinitely far away from its current locus of attention by annotating every intervening node in the stack with the antecedent's features. Note, incidentally, that we have no independent evidence for these particular

current cyclic, the explanation is circular: the Marcus parser simply could not analyze sentences involving successive cyclic wh-movement (and NP-movement) if only the current node were accessible for parsing rules. On further reflection, this is strange criticism indeed. The fact is that natural languages exhibit *wh*-movement and therefore the parser must have some way of encoding left context. Then, on the assumption that the human parser is a Marcus-type parser, certain properties of long distance movement are predicted, viz. that movement must be successive cyclic, because the parser cannot encode unbounded left context. The particular form of the locality contraint that governs overt movement is further determined by properties of the grammar.

In addition to this, Fodor (1985) points out that the fact that it is S that bounds access to the stack is quite arbitrary from the point of view of this kind of parser. On her view, we would only really have a functional explanation of subjacency if it could be shown to follow from the deterministic nature of the parser that it is S which bounds access to the stack rather than AP. It seems to me that Fodor is just asking for too much.

[45]As was first observed by Neijt (1979), gapping is subject to bounding conditions resembling subjacency. Berwick and Weinberg point out that this is exactly what one would expect, because a gapped verb leads to attachment ambiguities for a PP that follows the gap. Therefore, the parser must have access to the antecedent of the gapped verb and we expect subjacency to hold.

features from the domain of the grammatical theory implemented by this parser[46].

We will have to say a little bit more, however. It must be guaranteed that only a finite number of feature annotations are possible, or the number of features on the current could become arbitrarily large. This would make it impossible to encode the subtree attached to an active node as a single complex stack symbol in the parser's (finite) control[47]. In Marcus's terminology this can be understood as follows. Upon completion of a node, the parser would have to activate a different rule packet for every value of x, where x is the number of antecedents contained in the current. Since x could be arbitrarily large, the number of rule packets for encoding antecedents would have to be arbitrarily large.

In their presentation of the functional derivation of Subjacency, Berwick and Weinberg evade this problem by assuming a parsing equivalent of comp-to-comp movement in conjunction with a bounded search procedure that checks the first comp in the stack whenever the parser has to decide whether to insert a trace or not. Because every clause has exactly one comp, the question of how the number of locally accessible antecedents can be limited to just one does not seem to present itself. However, given the possibility of feature annotations using extragrammatical features, the local S'-node could of course be annotated with the features of other antecedents[48], which would void the functional derivation of Subjacency completely.

Now observe that the "no counting" argument can be used to solve this problem. We must somehow impose a bound on the number of antecedents that the parser can encode so as to guarantee that the current node will always be literally finite. If grammars cannot count, or rather can only count to one, then the only restriction on the number of encoded antecedents that can be written

---

[46]The issue of the linguistic motivation of the features that the parser uses is a thorny one that is directly related to the central topic of chapter 2, the relation grammar-parser. What is intended here is that the feature annotation technique is not in a one-one correspondence with the landing site theory of the grammar implemented by the parser. We will return to this matter in chapter 3.

[47]That complex symbol formation is possible at all depends on the fact that only the immediate daughters of the current can affect the parse. See Berwick (1985:pp.315ff.) for discussion.

[48]Since both Parsifal and Berwick and Weinberg's revised version of Parsifal use feature annotations that have no independent justification from the domain of the grammar realized by the parser, the theoretical possibility of feature annotations cannot be excluded on principled grounds.

in the vocabulary of the grammar is a restriction to just one[49]. In other words, the parser can only encode the *last* antecedent that it has come across. Notice that this is precisely the implication in the quote from Berwick (1985) above. Hence, given the no-counting argument, we cannot derive Subjacency in its entire scope, but we do derive the *Wh*-Island Condition.

In fact, the no-counting argument leaves just enough room for a very special type of *Wh*-Island violation. Given that the number of categorial features is finite, the parser could encode more than one antecedent, as long as the antecedents have different categorial features. This might explain the well known contrast below, which can only be observed in a preposition-stranding language such as English:

(47) (i) ? to $whom_i$ did you wonder [$_{CP}$ $what_j$ [$_{IP}$ PRO to [$_{VP}$ give t_j t_i]]]
(ii) * who_i did you wonder [$_{CP}$ $what_j$ [$_{IP}$ PRO to [$_{VP}$ give t_j to t_i]]]

Chomsky says about violations of the type (47ii):

> "As is well-known, these violations are much more severe than such examples as [(47i)], suggesting that some different factor is involved. One possibility is a version of the earliest proposal concerning these structures, namely, that double application of a rule to a given phrase is barred (see Chomsky 1964)."
> (Chomsky 1986a:p.39)

It would seem, then, that LRRL(k) parser could provide an elegant account for this otherwise mysterious ban on double application of a rule to a given phrase. However, the proposed account raises the question why (47i) or its degraded tensed equivalent should be less than perfect at all. We will return to this matter in chapter 3. Note, incidentally, that the bounded search alternative of Berwick and Weinberg, if at all available, does not distinguish between (47i) and (47ii), because it does not allow multiple encoding of any sort at all.

If this is correct, then the most that can be made to follow from LRRL(k) parser is the *Wh*-Island Condition[50], perhaps including some otherwise mysterious peculiarities. Subjacency in its full scope does not follow from an LRRL(k) parser. This drastically reduces the scope of the functional explanation that

---

[49]This discussion abstracts away from NP-movement cases. To be precise, then, as the grammar makes available the A/A'-distinction, the parser can encode exactly the presence of one antecedent in an A'-position and one antecedent in an A-position.

[50]Alternatively, we might say that we derive A'-minimality (cf. Rizzi 1987).

Berwick and Weinberg had in mind. In particular, we no longer explain why gapping should be bounded by Subjacency-like constraints (cf. fn.45), nor do we explain the noun complement case of the Complex Noun Phrase Constraint (CNPC):

(48) Complex NP Constraint
No element contained in a sentence dominated by a noun phrase with a lexical head noun may be moved out of that noun phrase by a transformation.
(Ross 1968:p.70)

To see this, bear in mind that the notion of bounding node no longer plays a role in the present functional explanation, at least not under its standard interpretation. Under the present analysis, an S-node is not a bounding node by stipulation, but derives this property from a conspiracy between a property of the parser (viz. that feature annotations must be finite) and a property of the grammar (viz. that grammars cannot count, or, alternatively, can only count to one). Therefore, the relative clause case of the CNPC *is* accounted for, because it is a *wh*-island.

2.7.3 Why GPSG combined with LRRL(k) parser explains Subjacency as well

Berwick and Weinberg claim that the functional derivation of Subjacency is impossible if we trade GB theory for GPSG. They begin their argument by pointing out that a GPSG posits a nonliteral representation of left context, the slash category notation[51], which makes an antecedent locally available at all

[51]The slash category notation encodes the presence of a *wh*-antecedent by means of the complex nonterminal XP/NP, where X is any category defined by the X'-system. The slashed category is eventually cashed out as an empty NP.

```
           QP/NP
          /     \
  who            S/NP
                /   \
          NP          VP/NP
          |          /  |  \
       Mary      V    NP      S/NP
                 |    |     /   |  \
              tell John that  NP  VP/NP
                              |   /   \
                           Bill liked NP/NP
                                        |
                                       [e]
```

times:

> "This information is available locally because the finitely representable (though complex) nonterminal label directly dominates the expansion site. Therefore the relevant parsing rules can all be finitely representable in a control table and all is well."
> (p.165)

They continue:

> ". . . a GPSG system could very well represent a parsing rule to handle this sentence:
>
> * Who do you wonder who remembers who likes?
>
> The first *who* would be encoded into slashed nonterminals as usual, carried along via the sequence QP/NP, VP/NP, and S/NP. Then the second *who* would be encountered, and passed along. Because there are now two nonterminals, this would have to be done by a context-free rewrite rule and complex nonterminal system such as, S'/NP→S/NP-1 NP-2, where NP-1 and NP-2 denote the first and second *who*s encountered, respectively. Next, the complex S would be expanded as an empty NP (corresponding to the missing subject NP filled by the second *who*) and VP/NP-1 (corresponding to the continued "transmission" of the first *who*). Then the third *who* would be picked up, and analyzed just like the second *who*; the first *who* would be passed along via a complex nonterminal VP/NP-1 as before. Finally, the object NP would be expanded as an empty element, with a rule like VP/NP-1→V NP[e]. Note that no problem would be encountered in carrying out the parse, no matter how far the first *wh*-constituent is from its argument position, and no matter how many complete S nodes with filled complementizer positions must be crossed."
> (p.166)

We will now demonstrate that this argument is completely misguided. For the slash category notation to be finitely representable, the number of slashes on a category must be finite, otherwise the grammar would contain an infinite number of categories and rewrite rules. It is therefore false to assume that an unrestricted slashed category system can be compiled into the finite control table of an LRRL(k) parser. It follows that an upper bound must be placed on the number of slashed categories that the grammar makes available. Given such a restriction, a GPSG could be implemented by an LRRL(k) parser. If we now invoke the no-counting argument for a GPSG implementation, just like Berwick and Weinberg did for their GB implementation, then the only restriction on the number of slashes on a category that can be stated in the rule writing vocabulary of the grammar is a restriction to just one. Therefore, we derive the *S/α,ß-filter of Chung & McCloskey (1983). This filter marks as ungrammatical any structure containing a clause from which more than one constituent has been extracted.

Since neither GB-theory nor GPSG can "count", we conclude that for both a GB-grammar and a GPSG there is a functional derivation of the *Wh*-Island Condition in terms of an LRRL(k) parser.

2.7.4 Summary of results

We may summarize this section as follows. LRRL(k) parsing requires a literally finite representation of left context. Consequently, there must be some bound on the number of antecedents that can be encoded on the current node. Given the assumption that natural grammars cannot count but can express the concept of adjacency (i.e. can count to one), we derive the basic result that the current node can be annotated with the features of one antecedent only. Hence, on the assumptions that the human parser is a variety of LRRL(k) parser and that natural grammars cannot count, we derive the *Wh*-Island Condition. Contrary to what Berwick and Weinberg (1984) claim, LRRL(k) parsers do not explain Subjacency, because the boundedness of phenomena that do not involve *wh*-islands remains unexplained. Finally, we have argued against Berwick and Weinberg (1984) that the functional derivations we have been considering are neutral between Government Binding Theory and GPSG.

2.8 Van de Koot (1987): barriers and determinism

In van de Koot (1987) I started from the fundamental idea that a functional explanation of Subjacency should be impossible in the absence of a coherent characterization of the boundedness property. As we have seen just now, this is not quite true: LRRL(k) parsing explains a subset of Subjacency phenomena (those that fall under the *Wh*-Island Condition) and this result does not depend upon a theory of bounding nodes. However, the idea still has content if we consider cases of the Complex Noun Phrase Condition, and still more so if we broaden the class of Subjacency facts to include extractions out of subjects and adjuncts, as is done in Chomsky's (1986a) *Barriers*. What I had in mind was that, once we had a coherent characterization of the boundedness property, we could try to tie that characterization to independently motivated properties of the parser. Therefore, I assumed the Barriers framework, as in that theory the boundedness property is not stipulated to hold of a particular subset of categories, but is instead defined in terms of L-marking[52]. The goal I set myself was to try to answer the question whether L-marking could be correlated to some property of deterministic parsing. This seemed feasible given the intuitive idea behind the barriers notation that movement is free out of licensed domains, where L-marking is understood as a form of licensing.

In what follows we will first familiarize ourselves with some basic properties of the Barriers framework. We then turn to an overview and a critical evaluation of the proposal in my paper.

2.8.1 Some basic properties of the Barriers framework

The Barriers theory relates government and Subjacency via the notion of a barrier. Simply put, an item cannot govern across a barrier and movement in the syntax cannot cross more than one barrier. Barrierhood is determined in a rather complex way, even though the generalization that Chomsky seeks to capture is rather straightforward: a maximal projection is a barrier unless it is a sister to a lexical item that assigns it a θ-role. Barrierhood, however, is defined via the notion of blocking category (BC).

Before we introduce any definitions, let us quickly repeat here the version of X'-theory that is adopted in the Barriers theory. Chomsky assumes a distinction between lexical and non-lexical categories, where the lexical categories are based on the features [αN,ßN], yielding the categories Noun ([+N,-V]), Verb ([-N,+V]), Adjective ([+N,+V]), and Preposition-Postposition ([-N,-V]). The nonlexical categories include complementizer and INFL. All other categories are projections of these zero-level categories in terms of the following universal schemata, where XP* stands for zero or more occurrences of some maximal projection. The order of sister categories is parametrized and is given here for English:

(49) (i) X' = X XP*
(ii) XP = XP* X'

Hence, we assume as before that the clausal categories S and S' are IP and CP,

---

[52]An introduction to the Barriers framework follows shortly.

respectively, where I=INFL and C=complementizer.

SpecIP is the position of the structural subject. Complementizers appear at the head of CP and *wh*-movement is to specCP. The head of CP is also the landing site for Aux-movement and V-movement (in languages like Dutch).

Let us now return to the definitions of Blocking Category (BC), L-marking and Barrierhood. A maximal projection α which dominates ß is a BC for ß if α is not L-marked (i.e. θ-marked by a lexical head). So in (50) below, for instance, the adjunct PP is a BC for the trace in specCP, because it is not θ-marked and therefore not L-marked either:

(50)
```
                 CP
                /     \
          what_i        C'
                       /   \
                     C       IP
                     |      /      \
                   did_k  IP          PP
                        /   \       /    \
                      NP     I'   P        CP
                      |     /  \ without  /   \
                     you   I    VP       t_i    C'
                           |   [______________]  /  \
                          t_k  to to London    C     IP
                                                  [_________]
                                                  reading t_i
```

Any BC, except IP, is automatically a barrier for ß and so is any maximal projection that immediately dominates α, α a BC. IP is "defective" and can only be a barrier by *inheritance* (cf. clause (a.) of the definition of barrierhood). So in the example above PP is not just a BC for the trace in specCP, it also a barrier. The IP dominating PP cannot be a barrier inherently, but it does inherit barrierhood from the BC that it directly dominates.

The relevant definitions are given directly below:

(51) Blocking Category
γ is a BC for ß iff γ is not L-marked and γ dominates ß

(52) L-marking
Where α is a lexical category, α L-marks ß iff ß agrees with the head of γ that is θ-governed by α

(53) Barrier
γ is a barrier for ß iff (a) or (b):
a. γ immediately dominates δ, δ a BC for ß
b. γ is a BC for ß, γ is not IP

The definition of L-marking introduces the relation of specifier-head agreement (henceforth SPEC-head agreement) to account for the extraction possibilities from subjects that are exceptionally case-marked. In its bare form SPEC-head agreement is the relation that holds between the subject of IP and the AGR element of I, but it is reinterpreted by Chomsky as a more abstract relation, viz. "the sharing of the features person, number, gender, case, etc. (the "ϕ-features" of Chomsky (198)1 and other work) when AGR is present and . . . sharing of an abstract ϕ-feature F when AGR is missing" (p.24).

If nothing else were said, however, this theory would block the best case of movement. Consider (54):

(54) What did [$_{IP}$John [$_{VP}$buy t]]

Chomsky assumes that I θ-marks VP, but since the head of IP is not lexical, the VP is not L-marked and is therefore a BC and a barrier. IP, which immediately dominates this BC now becomes a barrier by inheritance. Hence, movement of the object to its local specCP crosses two barriers and should be ungrammatical. Chomsky circumvents this problem by allowing adjunction to VP and by defining government in terms of exclusion:

(55) Exclusion
α excludes ß if no segment of α dominates ß

(56) Government
α governs ß iff α m-commands ß and there is no γ, γ a barrier for ß, such that γ excludes α

C-command is defined as follows:

(57) C-command
α c-commands ß iff α does not dominate ß and every δ that dominates α dominates ß

Where δ is restricted to maximal projections, we say that α m-commands ß.

Hence, (54) is assumed to have the structure (58):

(58) What did John $[_{VP}$ t'$[_{VP}$ buy t]]

Since the lower VP-segment, which is a BC and barrier, does not exclude *t'*, *t'* antecedent governs the object trace across this barrier. The upper VP-segment is not a BC for the adjoined trace, since it does not dominate that trace, where domination is defined as in (59) (Chomsky's (12)):

(59) Domination
α is dominated by ß only if it is dominated by every segment of ß

It should be obvious that the adjunction theory must be severely constrained or any barrier could be circumvented via adjunction. Therefore, a coherent adjunction theory is of vital importance to the plausibility of the Barriers theory, as has been pointed out by several critics of the model (e.g. Lightfoot and Weinberg 1988)[53]. So far, such a theory is still forthcoming[54].

To rehearse the concepts introduced sofar, consider the grammatical example below:

(60) who do you believe pictures of t to be on sale

The structure we have to consider is (61):

[53]For one thing, Lightfoot and Weinberg show that, contrary to what Chomsky argues, Superiority facts do not motivate adjunction to VP.

[54]Cf. Coopmans (1988) for a proposal that obviates some of these objections.

(61)
```
              CP
            /    \
       who_i      C'
                /    \
             do_k     IP
                    /    \
                  NP       I'
                  |      /    \
                 you    I      VP
                        |    /    \
                       t_k  t_i     VP
                                  /    \
                                 V       IP
                                 |     /    \
                            believe  NP       ...
                                   /    \
                                  N       PP
                                  |     /    \
                           pictures   P       NP
                                      |       |
                                      of      t_i
```

To see how the definitions of BC and barrierhood work, consider all maximal projections that are crossed by the movement from inside the subject NP to the VP-adjoined position. The PP-complement of *pictures* is L-marked (θ-marked by the lexical head *pictures*) and is therefore neither a BC nor a barrier for the trace internal to it. What about the NP dominating it? Is it L-marked? It is, because the lexical head *believe* θ-marks IP and the head of IP. It follows that the NP is L-marked as well, because it agrees with the head of IP (this demonstrates the importance of the relation called SPEC-head agreement). IP cannot be a barrier inherently, and because it does not directly dominate a maximal projection that is a BC, it does not inherit barrierhood either. The VP would have been a BC and a barrier if movement had crossed it (remember that I only θ-marks its VP-complement but does not L-mark it). But adjunction to VP voids barrierhood in the manner explained above. Now consider the second step: movement from the VP-adjoined position to specCP. VP is not a BC or a barrier for the trace adjoined to it, because not all of its segments dominate that trace. Because the VP is not a barrier, the IP dominating it cannot inherit barrierhood from it. Finally, IP cannot be a barrier inherently, so movement to specCP crosses no barriers at all.

Now consider the contrast below:

(62) (i) ? what$_i$ do you [t$_i$ [wonder how$_j$ to [t$_i$ [t$_j$ [repair t$_i$ t$_j$]]]]]
(ii) * how$_j$ do you [t$_j$ [wonder what$_i$ to [t$_j$ [t$_i$ [repair t$_i$ t$_j$]]]]]

According to Chomsky, sentence (62i) is a Subjacency violation, whereas (62ii) must in addition violate the ECP, as he concludes from its complete unacceptability[55]. In both sentences movement of the *wh*-element in the matrix clause has crossed one barrier. First the *wh*-element adjoins to the VP in the embedded clause, after which it moves in one swoop to the matrix VP and on to the matrix specCP. It is the movement from the lower VP to the matrix VP that crosses one barrier. Remember that IP is never a barrier inherently, but it is a BC because C does not L-mark the IP. Therefore CP inherits barrierhood from IP, unless movement is into specCP, which is impossible here, because that position is already occupied.

Now how does the Barriers model account for the contrast in (62)? Following Lasnik and Saito (1984), Chomsky assumes γ-marking as the mechanism for determining satisfaction of the ECP:

(63) γ-marking
  (i) α assigns the feature [+γ] to ß if it properly governs ß and ß receives the feature [-γ] if it is not properly governed
  (ii) a γ-feature, once assigned, is permanent
  (iii) γ-marking takes place at S-structure for elements of chains headed by argument-operators and at LF for elements of all other chains[56].

Proper government is defined as in (64):

(64) Proper government
  α properly governs ß iff α θ-governs or antecedent governs ß.

Antecedent government holds of a link (α,ß) of a chain, where α governs ß. The chain relation is expressed by coindexing. In order to avoid circularity, Chomsky defines θ-government in terms of sisterhood as follows:

(64) Θ-government
  α θ-governs ß iff α is a zero-level category that θ-marks ß, and α, ß are sisters.

The ECP can now be defined as in (65):

---

[55]Throughout *Barriers* rigid unacceptability is used as a diagnostic for ECP violations.

[56]In other words, gamma-marking at LF applies to all adjunct-operator chains, no matter whether they were created at S-structure or at LF, and to argument-operator chains created at LF.

(65) Empty Category Principle
[$_{NP}$e] must have the feature [+γ] at LF

From (63) it follows that the chains in (62) have the representation (66) at S-structure:

(66) (i) what$_i$ do you [$_{VP}$ t$_i$ [$_{VP}$ wonder [$_{CP}$ how$_j$ to
[+γ]
[$_{VP}$ t$_i$ [$_{VP}$ t$_j$ [$_{VP}$ repair t$_i$ t$_j$]]]]]]
[$-\gamma$] [+γ] [+γ][+γ]
(ii) how$_j$ do you [t$_j$ [wonder what$_i$ to [t$_j$ [t$_i$ [repair t$_i$ t$_j$]]]]]

Because *what* is an argument-operator, γ-marking for elements of its chain takes place at S-structure. The trace adjoined to the embedded VP is not antecedent governed: CP inherits barrierhood of IP, which is a BC for the adjoined trace. The adjunct-operator chain in (62ii) will not be γ-marked before LF (cf. 63iii). We may assume that the proposals outlined above imply the following ordering of processes at LF:

(67) (i) *wh*-raising[57]
(ii) free deletion of traces
(iii) γ-marking
(iv) γ-checking (i.e. the ECP)

For the chains in (66) this entails the following. The deletion rule deletes t_2 in (66i). Then γ-marking applies to the traces in chain (66ii) yielding (68) below:

(68) how$_j$ do you [$_{VP}$ t$_j$ [$_{VP}$ wonder [$_{CP}$ what$_i$ to
[+γ]
[$_{VP}$ t$_j$ [$_{VP}$ t$_i$ [$_{VP}$ repair t$_i$ t$_j$]]]]]]
[$-\gamma$] [+γ] [+γ][+γ]

Finally, the ECP (67iv) rules out the chain of the adjunct, because of the offending trace t_2. We see, then, that an offending intermediate trace in an S-structure argument-operator chain may be deleted at LF prior to γ-checking. Consequently, in the case of *wh*-movement from object position the intermediate traces are irrelevant for the ECP. Because the object trace is always properly

[57]At LF all *wh*-elements that have remained in situ in the mapping from D-structure to S-structure are moved to the position of an element that has undergone overt *wh*-movement. This rule of covert *wh*-movement is usually referred to as *wh*-raising.

governed by its θ-marking verb, all intermediate traces may be deleted at LF. It follows that *wh*-movement from object position will at most violate Subjacency. At LF movement from object position is always allowed, because the trace left behind will be θ-governed. For subjects, which are not properly governed by a θ-marking head, things are quite different. In the case of overt movement[58] the first chain link must satisfy the ECP. All other chain links need only satisfy Subjacency, because any offending traces may be deleted at LF. In the case of covert movement all chain links must satisfy the ECP, because an offending trace can no longer be deleted. Hence, in Chomsky's system subjects pattern with adjuncts at LF, as desired.

Let us now turn to Subjacency. Chomsky first defines n-Subjacency:

(69) n-Subjacency
ß is n-subjacent to α iff there are fewer than n+1 barriers for ß that exclude α

In the ideal case movement is 0-subjacent (i.e. crosses zero barriers). As we have seen 1-subjacent movement, as in (62i), still yields acceptable results. Subjacency is therefore defined as follows:

(70) Subjacency
If (α_i, α_{i+1}) is a link of a chain, then α_{i+1} is 1-subjacent to α_i

2.8.2 A review of the island violations

Let us now briefly review some standard island violations. Consider first the CED[59]. The CED cases fall into two classes usually referred to as the Subject Condition and the Adjunct Condition, illustrated in (71) and (72) respectively:

(71) (i) * the man who $[_{IP}[_{NP}$pictures of t] are on the table]
(ii) * the book that $[_{IP}[_{NP}$reading t] would be fun]
(72) (i) * to whom did $[_{IP}$they leave $[_{PP}$before speaking t]]
(ii) * who did $[_{IP}$ they leave $[_{PP}$before speaking to t]]

In (71) the embedded subject is not L-marked. It is therefore a BC and a barrier. IP, which directly dominates this BC, inherits barrierhood. Hence,

---

[58]I.e. movement in the mapping from D-structure to S-structure.

[59]Condition on Extraction Domains (Huang 1982).

movement has crossed two barriers and the sentence violates Subjacency. We do not get a stronger ECP violation at LF, because the foot of the chain is θ-governed and is hence γ-marked at S-structure. All intermediate traces may be deleted at LF. In (72) the adjunct is a BC and a barrier and, again, IP inherits barrierhood.

The adjunct island case of the CED yields a much stronger ECP violation if we extract an adjunct from an adjunct, as in (73):

(73) * how did you leave $[_{PP}$before fixing the car t]

Since for adjuncts γ-marking takes place at LF, all the links in an adjunct-operator chain must meet the antecedent government requirement at LF. It follows that (73) violates Subjacency at S-structure and the ECP at LF. Exactly the same is true of adjunct extraction from a subject:

(74) * how did $[_{IP}[_{NP}$reading the book t] please Mary

We now turn to violations of the Complex Noun Phrase Constraint (CNPC). Again, these fall into two categories: relative clause constructions and noun-complement constructions. As before I simply go through Chomsky's examples. Consider first extraction of an argument out of a relative clause (75i) and of an adjunct out of a relative clause (75ii):

(75) (i) * which book did John meet $[_{NP}$a child $[_{CP}$who read t]]
(ii) * how did John meet $[_{NP}$a man $[_{CP}$who fixed the car t]]

Here, too, we get a sharp contrast between extraction of an argument and extraction of an adjunct. In the latter case there is a much more extreme ECP violation. The relative clause is a BC and a barrier. The directly dominating NP inherits barrierhood, even though it is θ-governed itself. The noun complement cases in (76) below are similar to the relative clause cases, except that the island effect is somewhat weaker:

(76) (i) ? which book did John hear $[_{NP}$a rumor $[_{CP}$that you had read t]]
(ii) * how did John announce $[_{NP}$a plan $[_{CP}$ to fix the car t]]
(iii) how did $[_{IP}$ John $[_{VP}$ t_4 $[_{VP}$ announce $[_{NP}$ a plan $[_{CP}$ t_3 $[_{IP}$ PRO to $[_{VP}$ t_2 $[_{VP}$ fix the car t_1

As the unacceptability of (76ii) indicates, the construction must involve at least one barrier, otherwise we would not get an ECP violation in the case of extraction of an adjunct. But the intermediate status of (76i) suggests that either NP or CP is a barrier, but not both. In the Barriers system the ungrammaticality of (76ii) is attributed to the Minimality Condition. The idea here is that antecedent government of t_3 by t_4 in (76iii) is blocked by the intervening governor *plan*.

Finally, Chomsky's theory also accounts for wh-island violations:

(77) (i) * what$_i$ did you [t_i''[wonder [$_{CP}$ [to whom]$_k$ John [t_i'[gave t_i t_k]]]]]
(ii) * [to whom]$_k$ did you [t_k''[wonder [$_{CP}$ what$_i$ John [t_k'[gave t_i t_k]]]]]
(iii) ? what$_i$ did you [t_i''[wonder [$_{CP}$ [to whom]$_k$ to [t_i'[give t_i t_k]]]]]
(iv) ? [to whom]$_k$ did you [t_k''[wonder [$_{CP}$ what$_i$ to [t_k'[give t_i t_k]]]]]

In all cases in (77), movement from the adjoined position in the lower VP to the adjoined position in the matrix VP crosses one barrier: the embedded IP counts as a BC and hence the directly dominating CP inherits barrierhood. As one would expect, extraction of an adjunct out of a wh-island produces an ECP violation. Extraction from a tensed claused is somewhat worse than extraction from an infinitive, as is usual. This concludes our concise Barriers primer.

2.8.3 L-marking as a constraint on immediate attachment

Marcus (1980) uses the code "attach new vp-node to c as vp" to indicate the following sequence of parsing actions: (i) create a new vp-node, (ii) attach this newly created node to the current node and (iii) push this new (attached) vp-node on the stack as the new current. He remarks:

> "Normally, whenever a new node is created, as is done by the phrase "a new vp-node", the new node is pushed onto the active node stack immediately after its creation, immediately becoming a new current active node. If this were *always* true, however, there would be no way to immediately attach a newly created node to the current active node at the time of its creation. It would be necessary to always drop the new node into the buffer and only then attach it to the old (and once again) current active node."
> (p.80)

For this reason, Marcus introduces the construction *attach a new <type> node* *to c as <type>* with the interpretation given above[60]. For reasons I have not been able to uncover, Marcus only uses this construction to attach VP-nodes. Berwick and Weinberg do not use it at all. In their version of the Marcus parser a node is only attached after it has been fully completed.

The core of the proposal in my (1987) paper was to reintroduce Marcus's special code with full generality. The basic idea was that, by the Determinism Hypothesis, this type of attachment rule can only apply in cases in which the parser is absolutely sure about the proper attachment of a newly created node. The question that now had to be answered was what would license immediate attachment of a new node.

As a first move, I proposed to state a variant of L-marking more or less directly in the parser as a condition on immediate attachment. Immediate attachment rules would be constrained in such a way as to apply only under selection, where selection was understood as θ-marking by a head. For this to work properly, I had to make the further assumption that the heads of the nonlexical projections IP and CP select their complements as well, even though, as I pointed out, these may not be cases of θ-marking (Chomsky 1986a assumes that I, contrary to C, θ-marks its complement). Thirdly, I assumed that the selecting head itself must be lexical, where lexical must be understood as either (i) lexical and phonetic or (ii) carrying an index.

Having thus proposed something rather similar to L-marking as a condition on immediate attachment, I addressed the question to what extent these assumptions about the rule system of the parser could be independently motivated. I first argued that to assume θ-marking as a condition on immediate attachment rules is rather uncontroversial in terms of parsing theory, as it reflects the parser's adherence to the Projection Principle. Even though it may not be accurate to say that C and I *select* their complements, the presence of C unambiguously implies the presence of IP and the presence of I unambiguously implies the presence of VP. In an attempt to realize the Barriers theory as transparently as possible, I assumed that these logical relationships warrant direct attachment just in case the lexicality requirement is met as well. Finally, what about the requirement that the selecting head itself must be lexical (with the qualifications mentioned)? Weinberg, Aoun, Hornstein and Lightfoot (1987) require traces to be governed by a lexical head at PF. From this I speculated that head government should be construed as a parsing constraint, because trace insertion involves a parsing decision. In other words, I argued that

---

[60]It should be noted that are no compelling reasons for this proposal. Marcus (personal communication) confirms this.

the parser's decision to create a trace is dependent upon the presence of a lexical governor. I then suggested that perhaps the condition of head government applies to other parsing decisions as well, in particular to the decision to attach a newly created node.

As a result of the proposed generalization of the immediate attachment rule type, the stack representations differ considerably from the ones built by the original Marcus parser. Successive nodes in the stack may or may not be attached to each other, thus giving rise to sequences of attached stack elements.

Then, having stated the criteria for immediate attachment of a new node, I defined Domain as in (78), Current Domain as in (79) and Stack Accessibility as in (80):

(78) Domain
A domain is a maximal sequence of attached stack elements.

(79) Current Domain
The current domain is the maximal sequence of attached stack elements that includes the current node.

(80) Stack Accessibility
A constituent in the active node stack is transparent for parsing rules if and only if that constituent is part of the current domain.

I also proposed a very general trace insertion rule, which applies whenever insertion has a well-formed result[61]. The trace insertion rule creates a coindexed trace and drops it in the first cell of the buffer. A trace, once created, is attached in an A-position if that is required by the projection Principle and does not violate any constraints, otherwise it is Chomsky-adjoined to the current.

I assumed trace insertion to be illicit (i) if the current domain does not contain a proper antecedent, (ii) if it violates the θ-criterion, where I followed Chomsky's (1986a) suggestion that the configuration $[_{\alpha}\ X^{max}\ [_{\beta} \ldots]]$, where α=ß and ß is an argument, violates the θ-criterion, ß being invisible for θ-marking, and (iii) if the insertion site is ungoverned, where government is defined as (the parser's version of) government by an adjacent head. Here I assumed, following Kayne (1984), that V can govern an NP across a CP boundary[62]. This last

[61]I.e. whenever dropping a trace in the buffer does not violate any constraint in the system.

[62]I.e. an NP in specCP.

condition excludes insertion of a trace for the spec of an adjunct CP[63]. It follows that traces may be inserted in governed specCP positions and Chomsky-adjoined to non-arguments, if these non-arguments occupy governed positions[64].

Further, I assumed that every time the parser closes a domain which contains an antecedent, it drops a trace for subsequent attachment at the beginning of the new current domain. The head of IP not being a lexical head, VP is a barrier for movement to COMP, unless there is adjunction to VP first. How does the parser force movement through specCP? First, consider movement out of a θ-marked clause. In such a case, CP is not a barrier. However, C is not a lexical head and hence IP cannot be directly attached. I therefore assumed that C carries an index just in case specCP carries an index (i.e. I assumed spec-head agreement in CP). It follows from these assumptions that the barrierhood of IP is voided by movement to specCP. As a result of this movement, C gets an index and becomes lexical. What does this mean in terms of parsing? If the parser can drop a trace in the spec of CP, then IP does not count as a barrier, as it can be directly attached. Otherwise IP counts as a barrier. Second, consider movement out of an adjunct clause. As the CP is not θ-marked by a lexical head, the parser cannot directly attach it. Moreover, adjunct CPs occur in ungoverned (or unselected, cf. fn. 62) positions. Hence, the parser cannot insert a trace in the spec of CP, the new current domain. It follows that CP is a barrier in such cases. As specCP does not contain an index, SPEC-head agreement does not apply, C remains unindexed and barrierhood of IP cannot be voided. Hence, IP is a barrier as well.

I claimed that, as a result of the proposed revisions, the parser accounts for the subcases of bounding reduced to Subjacency in Chomsky (1986a). Insofar as the modified parser's variant of L-marking (i.e. the above assumptions concerning the conditions on the immediate attachment rule type and trace insertion) can be motivated on the basis of the Determinism Hypothesis, the parsing model seemed to explain these subcases of the Subjacency.

The Adjunct Condition follows from the proposed model, as adjuncts cannot be attached at the moment of their creation and the parser is unable to insert a trace in the adjunct's specCP position. Hence, the parser cannot insert a trace

---

[63]If adjunct CPs may sometimes occur in governed positions, then the stronger requirement of selection (in the broad sense adopted above) may be more appropriate.

[64]Note that while I assumed immediate attachment to be constrained by head government, trace insertion was assumed to be constrained by the weaker condition of government. We return to this matter in the critical discussion that follows this section.

within an adjunct, because the current domain will not contain an antecedent. The same holds for the Subject Condition. Consider (81) below:

(81) * the man $[_{CP}$who $[_{IP}[_{NP}$pictures of t] are on the table]]

At the point where the parser must create the trace in (81), its current domain is the subject NP. As the NP is not θ-marked by a lexical head, it cannot be attached at the moment of its creation. Also, the parser cannot adjoin a trace to the NP, as it is an argument. Therefore, the subject NP does not contain an antecedent for the trace internal to it.

As for the CNPC cases, relative clause CPs are not θ-marked and therefore cannot be directly attached. Given that adjunction to CP is barred, the relative clause is an island as required. The noun-complement construction remains a problem. The head noun θ-marks the CP that follows it, there is no *wh*-Island effect and the parser produces a well-formed output. Note, however, that it does not make much sense to blame this on the proposed model. In *Barriers* the intermediate status of extraction out of noun complements is a problem as well. In the absence of a clear grammatical characterization of the construction, one cannot expect the parser to behave any better than the grammar.

Finally, consider the wh-island violations in (82):

(82) (i) * what$_i$ did you wonder $[_{CP}$ [to whom]$_k$ John gave t_i t_k]
(ii) * [to whom]$_k$ did you wonder $[_{CP}$ what$_i$ John gave t_i t_k]
(iii) ? what$_i$ did you wonder $[_{CP}$ [to whom]$_k$ to give t_i t_k]
(iv) ? [to whom]$_k$ did you wonder $[_{CP}$ what$_i$ to give t_i t_k]

These data are problematic for the proposed analysis. Given that the embedded specCP contains an index (which I assumed appears on the head of CP as well, via SPEC-head agreement), the embedded IP can be attached at the moment of its creation. This will make both the embedded specCP and the matrix VP accessible to parsing rules at the moment the parser must create the embedded VP. Hence, the parser might be able to close the current domain by postulating two traces at the beginning of the new current domain (the embedded VP). Hence, one would have to make one of two assumptions. Either one assumes that a local antecedent turns the rest of the current domain opaque to further inspection or it is impossible to c-adjoin to VP twice. I left the choice between these assumptions as a topic for further investigation.

2.8.4 Criticism

The above proposal contains several weaknesses.

First, while direct attachment is contingent upon head government, the insertion of traces is only constrained by the weaker requirement of government. This seems to undermine the logic of the approach, because it destroys the connection between head government and trace creation. Once that connection disappears, the presence of the head government requirement as a constraint on direct attachment can no longer be understood as an adaptation to the exigencies of deterministic gap detection.

Second, the proposal fails to discriminate between ECP-violations and Subjacency violations. Consider the examples below:

(83) (i) * What did you go to London [without reading t]
(ii) * Why did you go to London [without reading a guide t]

In the Barriers model (83i) is a Subjacency violation and (83ii) is an ECP-violation. Now notice that the parser we are considering fails to drop a trace in (83i,ii) for exactly the same reason: there is no antecedent in the current domain (in both cases the adjunct is the current domain for the trace indicated). The combined effect of the antecedent requirement and the way the model restricts the accessibility of the stack is deadly here[65].

It is hard to see how the lexicality requirement for a governing head can be tied to determinism. Why should it be the case that mere selection (in the broad sense) does not suffice? The proposal does not answer this question.

The definition of stack accessibility (80) implies that there will be cases in which a potentially unbounded left context must be searched for an antecedent. However, this shortcoming can easily be taken care of by resorting to annotation of the current, as discussed in section 2.7.2.

Finally, the proposed model does not incorporate the notion of inheritance (see 53a above). It therefore does not distinguish between mild and strong Subjacency violations. The concept of "inheritance" is strictly unamenable to processing, simply because a node that inherits barrierhood has already been analyzed when the parser builds the node that it inherits barrierhood from. It does not follow from this that either the grammar or the parser is wrong, but simply that inherited barrierhood cannot be straightforwardly represented in the

[65]Notice that the antecedent requirement is crucial and hence that one of the easy solutions to solve this problem, viz. to allow the parser to drop a trace in (82i) on the basis of selectional criteria, is unavailable.

parser in a way similar to ordinary barrierhood. We will not pursue this matter any further here.

2.9 Summary

We began this chapter with an overview of Marcus's parser, after which we discussed some apparent counterexamples to the lookahead mechanism, showing that a Marcus parser with lookahead makes better psycholinguistic predictions than a minimal commitment parser, if we assume that the use of lookahead is associated with ambiguities that arise as a result of one lexical item being associated with more than one θ-grid.

Then, in sections 2.5 and 2.6, we first presented some of the modifications to the original Marcus parser proposed by Berwick and Weinberg and summarized their claims about what grammars can be parsed by this parser. It was then shown that these claim are incorrect: we reviewed Nozohoor-Farshi's (1986) demonstration that the Marcus parser can neither be modeled by a Bounded Context Parser, nor by an LR(k) parser. Instead, it turned out that the Marcus parser is a restricted LRRL(k) parser.

Section 2.7 investigated the explanatory potential of LRRL(k) parsing with respect to Subjacency. It was argued that LRRL(k) parsing only explains a subset of Subjacency phenomena, in particular the *Wh*-Island Condition. We also argued against Berwick and weinberg's (1984) claim that there is no functional derivation of Subjacency (or rather the *Wh*-Island Condition) in terms of LRRL(k) parsing for the GPSG framework, showing that the explanatory potential of LRRL(k) parsing is completely neutral between these competing grammatical theories on the reasonable assumption that if GB-grammars cannot count then neither can GPSGs.

Finally, section 2.8 turned to a dicussion of my (1987) paper "On Explaining Subjacency". We began by presenting a concise summary of the Barriers framework (Chomsky 1986a), after which we reviewed my proposal to treat L-marking as a parsing condition on immediate attachment of newly created incomplete phrases. It was shown that this proposal suffers from a number of serious conceptual and empirical defects.

In the following chapter it will be argued that some of the key ideas in my (1987) paper can be made to work after after all, if we take a rather different view of attachment decisions in deterministic parsers.

Chapter 3

Grammatical Constraints and Determinism

3.1 Preview

At the end of chapter 1 we concluded that the Natural Computation Framework accords a prominent role to competence theories in AI models of cognitive functions, because it insists on an approach that puts the structure of the information-processing problem in the focus of attention. One might be tempted to conclude from this that, since competence theories are a necessary prerequisite to the development of algorithmic theories, algorithmic theories can be of no importance in the development of competence theories. This conclusion is not warranted, however. One could very well imagine a situation in which a well-developed competence theory could profit from insights gained from a particular algorithmic realization of that theory. That is, if one is prepared to acknowledge that such insights are at best suggestive and require independent motivation at the level of the competence theory. If the insights from the algorithmic theory suggest modifications that are empirically neutral, then, to the extent that we have independent evidence for the particular algorithm that we use, we should welcome these results, because, all other things being equal, we clearly prefer the simplest possible relationship between the competence theory and the algorithmic theory.

In this chapter we develop an informal chain algorithm for the runtime grammar of the original Marcus parser. The resulting parser produces outputs that are not always transparently related to the corresponding structures generated by the competence grammar. The assumed competence grammar (the Barriers theory) leans rather heavily on a number of stipulations concerning adjunction, which are tacitly assumed to be derivable from a sofar non-existent theory of adjunction. As it turns out, the runtime grammar we develop accounts for many of the data that the competence theory accounts for without recourse to these stipulations. In fact, the runtime grammar allows adjunction to any XP, but crucially disallows multiple adjunction. This restriction echoes an important result of the previous chapter: given the assumptions that grammars cannot count, a grammar that allows multiple adjunction cannot be parsed by the particular parser that we use (an LRRL(k) parser).

The move to unrestricted adjunction (i.e. adjunction to any XP) is inspired by a desire to get rid of feature annotations for encoding the presence of an antecedent (see section 2.7.2 for discussion). Remember that there are no principled reasons for rejecting such feature annotations techniques. The competence grammar only specifies the function that the parser must compute, and tells us nothing about how the parser actually computes that function. However, the introduction of features that do not occur in the grammar weakens the relationship between the grammar and the parser. If we allow unrestricted adjunction in the runtime grammar, the parser can use traces (instead of such features) to encode the presence of an antecedent, while there is no need for auxiliary assumption about the accessibility of the stack for parsing rules.

In what follows the primary focus will be on the development of the runtime grammar and on how it accounts for the data. In chapter 4 we evaluate the competence grammar against the runtime grammar, suggesting ways to increase the grammar-parser equivalence.

Because these suggestions are the result of specific assumptions about the nature of the human sentence processor (specifically that it is a restricted LRRL(k) parser), for which we have only circumstantial independent motivation, they are at once highly speculative and of great explanatory value if correct. This is so, because certain properties of syntactic movement can be directly linked to the exigencies of deterministic parsing and are in that sense explained by the assumption of determinism.

Let us briefly summarize our position:

- We start from the hypothesis that the human parser is a restricted LRRL(k) parser. We know that this hypothesis is not at all necessarily true, but will value it in proportion to the insights that we gain from it.
- The parser uses traces instead of feature annotations that are unmotivated from the point of view of Government Binding Theory.
- All other things being equal, we prefer the simplest possible relationship between the grammar and the parser. This implies that we should welcome modifications of the grammar based on insights from the domain of parsing to the extent that these modifications do not weaken the descriptive or explanatory capacity of the grammar.

This chapter is organized as follows. Section 3.2 shows that an LRRL(k) parser that does not use feature annotations that are unmotivated from the point of view of the grammar that the parser implements enforces a very strict locality constraint on syntactic movement. In section 3.3 we develop criteria for deterministic chain formation, arguing that information about the θ-marking properties and the subcategorization frames of lexical items in the parser's lexicon plays a key role in licensing the attachment site of completed constituents. We propose a contrast between licensed and unlicensed attachment, showing how such a contrast can shed light on the existence of certain constraints on syntactic movement. A key feature of the proposed analysis is that it exposes a fundamental symmetry between the CED and the parasitic gap construction. We summarize our findings in section 3.4.

3.2 LRRL(k) parsing and locality in chains

3.2.1 The analysis of wh-movement

In section 2.7.2 we discussed how an LRRL(k) parser can use linguistically unmotivated feature annotations to encode the presence of an antecedent. We will now investigate the hypothesis that the parser uses traces instead of feature annotations. In addition, we make no auxiliary assumptions about the accessibility of the parser's stack: i.e. only the current node and its immediate daughters are accessible for parsing rules. Given that only the current node is accessible, we must allow adjunction to any XP or it will be impossible to encode the presence of an antecedent across an unbounded distance. It follows from these assumptions that a simple case of *wh*-movement like (1i) will be assigned the structure (1ii):

(1) (i) who did John kiss?
(ii) who_i did $[_{IP}$ t_i $[_{IP}$ John $[_{VP}$ t_i $[_{VP}$ kiss $t_i]]]]$

In other words, the only one way in which the parser can encode the presence of an antecedent is by adjoining a trace to every maximal projection c-commanded by the antecedent, until a gap is detected.

3.2.2 Traces versus features: antecedent government

The assumption that the parser does not use feature annotation to encode the presence of an antecedent raises a serious problem with respect to A-chains. Consider a standard case of NP-movement:

(2) John was believed $[_{IP}$t' to have been $[_{VP}$kidnapped t]]

NP-movement is not assumed to leave a trace in every maximal projection that intervenes between the head and the foot of the chain. In terms of our parser this has the undesirable consequence that neither of the two traces indicated in (2) has an accessible antecedent at the point where it should be created. It should be noted that, while we could solve this problem by allowing feature annotation on the intervening VP-nodes, we would create a new problem as well, because there would be no way to exclude cases of super-raising or super-passive:

(3) (i) * [John [seems [that [it is [certain [t to win]]]]]]
(ii) * [John [seems [that [it was [killed t]]]]]

In order to obviate these problems, suppose we assume (i) that the parser uses traces only, (ii) that the SPEC of VP and the SPEC of AP are A-positions, and (iii) that adjoined positions are A'-positions, as is standard. The second of these assumptions is based on the idea that the position of subjects at D-structure is specVP universally, as has been proposed by Kuroda (1986)[66]. Kuroda points out that the conceptual simplification that results from including the expansion of C and I in the general X'-schema is considerably weakened by the fact that the category V conforms only defectively to the schema of the extended X'-theory. His paper investigates the consequences of the conceptually simplest assumption, viz. that specVP is the D-structure subject position, with some elegant results.

Suppose we make the above assumptions. Furthermore, let us abstract away for the time being from the possibility of intervening barriers, choosing instead to think of chain formation from a pure parsing perspective. That is, we think of chain formation as a parsing process that is constrained by the presence or absence of a proper antecedent. We now kill two birds with one stone. Given the above assumptions about specVP, the parser will be able to construct a proper chain for NP-movement cases, because in cases where raising or passive is possible specVP/specAP is a θ-bar position:

(4) (i) [$_{IP}$John was [$_{VP}$t killed t]]
(ii) [$_{IP}$John [$_{VP}$t seems [$_{IP}$t to [$_{VP}$t win]]]
(iii) [$_{IP}$John [$_{VP}$t is [$_{AP}$t likely [$_{IP}$t to [$_{VP}$t die]]]]

Second, super-raising and super-passive are excluded for two independent reasons:

(5) (i) * [$_{IP}$John [$_{VP}t_i$ seems [$_{CP}$(t_i) that [$_{IP}$it [$_{VP}t_i$ is [$_{AP}t_i$ certain [$_{IP}t_i$ to [$_{VP}t_i$ win]]]]]]]]
(ii) * [$_{IP}$John [$_{VP}t_i$ seems [$_{CP}$(t_i) that [$_{IP}$it [$_{VP}t_i$ was [$_{AP}t_i$ killed t_i]]]]]]

---

[66]Koopman and Sportiche (1985) propose an analysis that is rather similar to Kuroda's, except that in their view the D-structure subject is generated in a VP-adjoined position, i.e. it is the subject of a small clause.

First, in both (5i,ii) a C-projection intervenes, which does not have an A-position. Hence, chain formation is blocked and both sentences are ruled out. Second, in both (5i,ii) one of the intermediate positions (specIP) is filled, effectively blocking chain formation. I.e., we assume that chain links are coindexed at the moment of their creation. Hence, a dummy element like *it* cannot be coindexed with a governing trace, as it is part of the parser's input and not a created chain link[67].

This analysis of NP-movement has some very interesting consequences in connection with the debate whether the locality condition on traces in A-chains should be accounted for by the Binding Theory (henceforth BT) or by the ECP.

As has been noted by many people, reducing the ECP to antecedent government leads to serious overlap with the BT in the case of A-chains. In (2) both the ECP and the BT require *John* and *t'*, and *t'* and *t* to be locally coindexed. Since the locality requirement imposed on traces of NP-movement appears to follow independently from the BT, it has been suggested that maybe the ECP should not apply to traces of NP-movement. There is some evidence, however, that the ECP should apply to these traces anyway[68].

Chomsky (1986a) argues that (3i) cannot be excluded by the BT and that therefore it must be an ECP violation. The point he raises is that *it* is not an accessible subject for the trace in this case, as coindexing of the trace and *it* would yield an i-within-i violation[69]. Hence, the root clause is the Governing Category for *t* and the sentence does not violate the BT. By contrast, the ECP requires that *John* antecedent governs its trace in (3i), because *certain* governs but does not properly govern the trace of *John*. Since antecedent government is blocked (at least) by CP, (3i) is ruled out, as required.

Lasnik (1985) argues that a condition like (6) below is necessary anyhow to rule out sentences like (7):

---

[67]It is, we bar accidental coindexing.

[68]Apart from the evidence against the assumption that the BT suffices to account for the locality requirements on traces of NP-movement discussed below, there is the further problem that the locality of NP-movement is not subject to parametric variation, whereas such variation does seem to exist in the case of binding of overt anaphors.

[69]The i-within-i condition (Chomsky 1981) may be stated as follows:

*$[_{\alpha}...\beta...]$, where α and β bear the same index

This well-formedness condition rules out phrases like the ones below:

- * $[_{NP_i}$the friends of $[_i$each other's$]$ parents$]$
- * There is $[_{NP_i}$a picture of $[_{NP_i}$itself$]]$ on the mantelpiece

(6) If α_i and α_{i+1} are successive links in an A/A'-chain, then α_i locally A/A'-binds α_{i+1}.

(7) * John$_i$ is believed [(that) [he$_i$ is proud t$_i$]]

In (7) the θ-criterion demands that there be two chains (John$_i$,t$_i$) and (he$_i$). Since *proud* θ-governs the trace of John, one would expect (7) to be no worse than a (weak) Subjacency violation. Its severe ungrammaticality suggests that it must be an ECP violation after all. It would therefore seem that θ-government does not suffice for proper government of an A-bound trace. Now observe that while Lasnik's binding condition has the desired effect in (7), it fails to account for the ungrammaticality of example (3i) above, because the trace is locally A-bound by *John*. Therefore, the extra condition on A-bound traces must not be local binding but antecedent government. This is exactly the possibility that is explored in *Barriers* (see chapter 11 of that work for discussion) and which leads Chomsky to the conclusion that for a wide range of cases the ECP can be reduced to antecedent government and treated as a chain phenomenon.

Let us now consider how our parser excludes (7). The only way the parser can construct a chain for an NP-moved constituent is by dropping a trace in every specifier position that intervenes between the antecedent and the gap. Hence, some version of antecedent government is in effect enforced by the chain algorithm that the parser incorporates[70]. Because neither the C-projection nor the I-projection has an A-position that can be used for chain formation, there is clearly no way for the parser to derive (7).

3.2.3 Towards a generalized condition on chain links: wh-islands

The way the parser accounts for (7) is quite similar to the account of *wh*-islands discussed in chapter 2. Consider again a typical case:

(8) * to whom did you wonder what John gave

An LRRL(k) parser that uses traces explains the *Wh*-Island Condition in exactly the same way as one that uses feature annotation. Remember that the relevant restriction is that an LRRL(k) parser can only encode a finite number of antecedents. In section 2.7.2, we argued that the only restriction on the number

[70]We will define proper government shortly.

of antecedents that can be stated in the vocabulary of the grammar is a restriction to just one (see section 2.7.2 for details). Hence, chain formation will fail for one of the two chains in (8), because the parser cannot adjoin two traces to the embedded IP.

However, things are slightly more complex and merit additional discussion, even though the basic result stands. The point is that there are two slightly different ways to state the restriction on the encoding of antecedents, which might have different empirical consequences, depending on further theoretical assumptions.

First, and this is the option we have sofar pursued, we could exclude multiple adjunction to any XP. This radically excludes any *wh*-island violation, because it is impossible to encode more than one antecedent at any point in the parse.

Second, we could just exclude adjunction to CP. This would exclude any *wh*-island violation, at least under the standard analysis. But at the same time, it opens up possibilities for an alternative analysis of infinitival *wh*-islands that could provide an account for their relative acceptability.

We have assumed, following Kuroda (1986), that the D-structure position of subjects is specVP. We could therefore assume that PRO, the subject of an infinitive, remains in its D-structure position. Then, on the assumption that specIP could be an A'-position in these cases, that position would be available as a landing site for *wh*-movement, leaving specCP available for cyclic movement[71]. Under this analysis, infinitival *wh*-islands would have the S-structure (9):

(9) ? what$_i$ did [$_{IP}$t$_i$ [$_{IP}$you [$_{VP}$t$_i$ [$_{VP}$wonder [$_{CP}$t$_i$ [$_{IP}$t$_i$ [$_{IP}$ [to whom]$_k$ to [$_{VP}$t$_k$ [$_{VP}$t$_i$ [$_{VP}$PRO give t$_i$ t$_k$]]]]]]]]]]

The crucial step in the parser's analysis of (9) is the double adjunction to the embedded VP. At that point both the trace adjoined to IP and the *wh*-element in the spec of IP are current and hence accessible to the parser's rules. So all is well.

Even though Kuroda's proposal seems to have about the right consequences here, one might wonder what causes the slightly degraded status of such

[71]Admittedly, this idea is highly speculative in the absence of a coherent proposal about the status of specIP.

examples as (9). The question takes on urgency if we consider (10)[72]:

(10) (i) * how do you wonder what to repair
(ii) how$_j$ do [$_{IP}$t$_j$ [$_{IP}$you [$_{VP}$t$_j$ [$_{VP}$wonder[$_{CP}$t$_j$ [$_{IP}$t$_j$ [$_{IP}$what$_i$ to [$_{VP}$t$_j$ [$_{VP}$t$_i$ [$_{VP}$PRO repair t$_i$]]]]]]]]]]

Adjunct extraction from an infinitival *wh*-complement is completely unacceptable. This would follow if we assumed (i) that the *wh*-element in specIP must move to specCP at LF and (ii) that chains of adjunct-operator movement must remain intact in the mapping to LF, as would be required under the Barriers theory (we will cover this topic in more detail in section 3.3.4). Under this scenario the degraded status of (9) could perhaps be attributed to a failure to satisfy the selectional restriction of *wonder* at S-structure.

There are other problems with the analysis in (9), which are quite independent of our proposal. It seems that infinitival *wh*-islands are only transparent for "local" arguments. Consider (11):

(11) * who do you wonder to whom to tell that John hit

Needless to say, none of these complications will occur if we discard the idea that specIP can be an A'-position, although that would leave unsolved the problem of the relative acceptability of infinitival *wh*-islands.

No matter which way we choose to state the restriction on adjunction, the parser's account of the unacceptability of certain *wh*-islands is quite identical to how it rules out super-raising and super-passive. In all cases it comes across an element in the input that breaks up the chain that is being constructed. We tentatively conclude from this that the parser behaves in accordance with what Sportiche (1989) has referred to as the Condition on Chain Links (henceforth: CCL):

(12) Condition on Chain Links (CCL)
A trace must be antecedent governed

Our version of the CCL is more restrictive than Sportiche's, however, because of the way we define antecedent government (13), where Domination and Exclusion are defined as in 2.8.1 (59) and (55), which we repeat below for

---

[72]We assume that the D-structure position of adjuncts is a VP-adjoined position (or perhaps an IP-adjoined position in some cases). We will return to this matter later. For now we simply assume it.

convenience (cf. Chomsky 1986a):

(13) Antecedent Government
α antecedent governs ß iff
(i) a category δ that directly dominates γ, δ and γ not of the same category and γ a maximal category directly dominating ß, does not exclude α, and
(ii) α and ß are members of the same chain

(14) Domination
α is dominated by ß only if it is dominated by every segment of ß

(15) Exclusion
α excludes ß if no segment of α dominates ß

Even though the intuition underlying this version of antecedent government is quite simple, its definition is rather complex, because it has to accommodate the cases below:

```
(16)   (i)    \                       (ii)    \
               δ                               δ
             /   \                           /   \
            α     δ                         α     δ
                 / \                             / \
                    γ                               γ
                  /   \                            / \
                 ß     γ                          β   σ

       (iii)    \                     (iv) *    \
                 δ                               σ
               /   \                           /   \
              α     δ                         α     σ
                   / \                             / \
                      γ                               δ
                    /   \                           /   \
                   γ                                     γ
                 /   \                                  / \
                β     γ                                β
```

```
(vi)     \
          δ
        /   \
       α     γ
            /
          β
```

We will assume a complex parsing action *adjoin* that builds adjunction structures. For instance, after a trace has been adjoined to a (current) VP, the current will have the following configuration:

```
(17)          VP
             / \
            t   VP
```

We are now in a position to define the parser's equivalent of antecedent government as a particular machine configuration, namely the configuration in which the creation of a trace is licensed by an antecedent that is an immediate daughter of the current. We define *immediate daughter* as in (18):

(18) Immediate Daughter
A node α is an immediate daughter of a node ß iff it is directly dominated by a segment of ß

This definition has the effect of making accessible to parsing rules all the nodes adjoined to a node α as well as the nodes directly dominated by the lowest segment of α.

Notice that antecedent government is a necessary condition on trace creation but need not be a sufficient condition. In fact, we will see later on that there are cases in which it is insufficient. We will assume that the creation of a trace involves coindexation with its antecedent. Hence, the second clause of the definition of antecedent government is reflected in the parser's operations as well.

The reader should bear in mind that the parser we are considering builds an S-structure. Therefore, when we say that the parser behaves in accordance with the CCL, we mean to say that it realizes a grammar that observes the CCL in its mapping from D-structure to S-structure. Whether the mapping from S-structure to LF observes the CCL as well remains an open question for now. In our terms, the answer would be dependent upon properties of the algorithm that maps S-structures into LF-representations and is beyond the scope of the present investigation.

3.2.4 Adjunction and grammar size

Weinberg (1988) claims that the addition of the "slashed category" notation to a grammar renders recognition of strings generated by that grammar computationally intractable. Although she does not present any arguments to support this claim, she refers to Berwick & Weinberg (1984) and Barton, Berwick & Ristad (1987) for a proof of this result. As it would seem that the proposal to allow unrestricted adjunction to all maximal categories comes close to a notational variant of the "slashed category" notation, Weinberg's claim merits some discussion.

First, the slashed category notation does not *in and of itself* cause intractability, as is confirmed by Ristad (personal communication). He points out that things are more complicated than that because the slashed category notation is usually accompanied by other devices that do cause intractability. He gives the example of the GPSG version in Gazdar (1981), which uses slash categories that do not cause intractability because they simply square the number of possible nonterminals in an equivalent context-free grammar. The true source of complexity in that version of GPSG are the metarules, which can generate infinite rule sets and can allow the resulting grammar to generate undecidable languages. Even if the metarules are severely restricted, the universal recognition problem for these restricted GPSGs remains intractable[73].

Ristad continues that similar remarks are in order with respect to later versions of GPSG, where the real problem is that categories are sets of features and no longer atomic symbols, as in Gazdar (1981), and that local trees are subject to feature agreement principles[74].

More generally, the possibility of adjunction does not increase the number of categories in the grammar. The most it will do is increase the number of rewrite rules. Suppose the grammar contained x rewrite rules and y categories. Then, if we allowed all categories to adjoin to all categories, we would increase the number of rewrite rules by the product of x and y, i.e. by a an amount linear in the number of categories.

---

[73]NP-hard, to be precise (cf. Barton, Berwick and Ristad 1987).

[74]The universal recognition problem for these versions of GPSG is EXPPOLY-hard (cf. Barton, Berwick and Ristad 1987).

3.3 Deterministic chain formation

3.3.1 Introduction

In the previous sections we have seen how some fairly simple properties of an LRRL(k) parser in conjunction with the restriction that grammars cannot count provide an explanation for *wh*-island phenomena and the strict locality constraint observed by NP-movement. In this section we will make an important second step. We begin by taking a closer look at deterministic chain formation. Criteria will be developed for deterministic attachment of completed phrases and deterministic creation of ECs. It will be shown how this constrained parser accounts for the unacceptability of *wh*-movement out of subjects (the Subject Condition) and adjuncts (the Adjunct Condition).

3.3.2 Adjunct attachment as a last resort strategy

When a Marcus-type parser completes a constituent, it pops it from the stack and drops it in the first cell of the buffer, after which it must be attached. Sometimes, however, deterministic parsers are faced with syntactic ambiguities for which, given just syntax, no disambiguation exists. One of these is the attachment ambiguity that arises with modifiers. Consider the following example:

(19) a boy sat in the leather chair [that had just arrived from New York]

Here the relative clause could very well modify either the subject or the object. As these options correspond to different attachment sites, the parser is confronted with an unresolvable syntactic ambiguity. The same is true of sentences with PP-attachment ambiguities:

(20) I saw a man on the hill with a telescope

Here *with a telescope* could either modify the verb or the object. Similarly, *on the hill* could either be a sentential adverbial or a postmodifier to *man*. Again these options correspond to different attachment sites and again, given just syntax, the parser can do nothing to disambiguate the sentence. Notice that these cases differ markedly from the sort of local ambiguities that we have discussed in connection with trace creation in chapter 2. In those cases, the ambiguity could be resolved on the basis of syntactic evidence.

In theory there are several ways of dealing with attachment ambiguities in deterministic parsers, but none are principled. One could, for instance, make sure that some ad hoc attachment strategy prevents the parser from halting in cases in which the attachment site is ambiguous. This is essentially the proposal of Miller and Chomsky (1963), who suggest that ambiguous adjuncts should be attached to the lowest node in the parse tree. Figuring out the appropriate reading(s) for these structures is then left to later semantic processes.

It should be noted that some attachment ambiguities can be resolved using phonological input. For instance, the two readings of (19) are associated with markedly different intonational patterns, partly related to focus. Still, one would like the parser to be able to handle these cases even in the absence of phonological input, because that is after all a task that human beings seem to perform fairly easily during reading.

Here we will opt for a solution that is rather similar to Miller and Chomsky's. To begin with, we follow their suggestion that ambiguous adjuncts should be attached to the lowest node in the parse tree. In addition, we assume that adjuncts cannot be attached as a sister to a head or as a specifier. Instead, we assume that adjuncts are exactly what their name says they are: i.e. they occupy adjunction positions. Let us therefore consider how we might extend the parser's runtime grammar to accommodate the attachment of adjuncts.

For ease of exposition let us first settle on a particular rule format for the parser. Since we have already discussed the grammar of the original Marcus parser, let us assume that our parser uses rule packets that are quite similar to the ones used in that parsing model. However, we discard the immediate attachment rule type that was used in that parser and in my (1987) paper, which we discussed in section 2.8.

We first discuss how the parser's grammar would have to be extended to accommodate the cases of trace-adjunction we have discussed. Whenever the parser is about to create a new constituent and to activate the appropriate rule packets to build that constituent, it must check if the current node contains an antecedent (i.e. a phrase in a θ-bar position). We define A-antecedent and A'-antecedent as follows:

(21) A-antecedent
An A-antecedent is a constituent in an A-position that is a θ-bar position

(22) A'-antecedent
An A'-antecedent is a constituent which is either in a position adjoined to some XP or in specCP

Suppose the current contains an antecedent, then the parser must activate an additional rule packet to handle the creation and attachment of a trace in the new constituent[75]. In fact, we will assume that the runtime grammar contains at least two such additional packets. The first of these is activated if the antecedent occupies an A'-position and the second if the antecedent occupies an A-position. Notice that both packets may be active simultaneously: after all, passive does not inhibit *wh*-movement or vice versa. For ease of reference let us give these packets the names A'-ANTECEDENT and A-ANTECEDENT.

It is quite beyond the scope of this work to write the actual rules that do the work of gap detection and trace attachment. The point is that each and every rule packet of the Marcus parser's runtime grammar must be rewritten to properly interact with the packets A-ANTECEDENT and A'-ANTECEDENT. To give an example, suppose the packet A'-ANTECEDENT and the hypothetical packet PARSE-IP are simultaneously active. Then the portion of PARSE-IP that parses the specifier of IP must first determine whether the specifier happens to be, say, a full NP sitting in the buffer awaiting attachment. Suppose this is the case, then it must call a rule in the packet A'-ANTECEDENT to create and adjoin a trace. This rule must then hand back control to the packet PARSE-IP, which may now parse the specifier. A second possibility would be that the buffer does not contain a specifier. Then the specifier could be either PRO or trace. Assume this can be tested by consulting the local environment of the parse (e.g. checking for (head) government or tense). If it must be trace, the packet PARSE-IP must call a rule in the packet A'-ANTECEDENT that creates and attaches the trace and hands back control to the packet PARSE-IP. If it must be PRO, some other line of action must be pursued. All the Marcus parser's major rule packets would have to be adapted to perform in this fashion. While this informal sketch may give the reader a feel of how this chain algorithm might be implemented in the Marcus parser, it should also be apparent that rewriting the parser's grammar is well beyond the present undertaking.

The next step is to extend the parser's grammar to accommodate the adjunction of non-arguments other than intermediate traces. How does the parser distinguish constituents that are complements to a head from those that are not? In order to pass for a complement, a constituent must subcategorize the current's

[75]It would be more appropriate to have the parser drop a trace in the buffer *before* the new node is created and the corresponding packets are activated, because only then could we truly speak of antecedent-dependent creation of traces. The present line of action, in which the trace is dropped in the buffer *after* the new node has been created, was chosen to avoid a number of technical difficulties that would have led to unnecessary complications in the presentation of the main line of argument. Nothing of crucial importance seems to hinge on the matter.

head[76]. Following standard practice, we assume that lexical entries contain both a subcategorization frame and a linked θ-grid. A θ-role in a grid that is not linked is an external θ-role. So, for instance, the verb *kiss* has the lexical entry (23):

(23) $[_V kiss]$: _ NP
$\quad\quad\quad\quad\quad\quad\;|$
$\quad\quad\quad\;(\theta_1,\theta_2)$

Adjunct attachment could now be implemented as follows. When the parser decides that the current node is complete, it must not immediately pop that constituent from the stack for subsequent attachment, but it must first parse any remaining adjunct material for subsequent adjunction to the complete constituent. Only after the stray adjunct material has been adjoined can the parser pop the complete constituent from the stack. This attachment strategy raises two problems.

First, it is based on the incorrect assumption that adjuncts wear their adjunct-status on their sleeves. The problem is that, given this attachment strategy, the parser might end up attaching a PP as an NP-internal adjunct, only to find out later that it should have analyzed that PP as a sister to the NP it has just attached. In other words, the material in the buffer might in actual fact be an argument of the phrase that directly dominates the NP. This type of attachment ambiguity differs from the cases discussed above in that here one of the attachment sites is *not* an adjunct attachment site. Hence, the ambiguity that occurs is local. Consider an example of this sort of local ambiguity:

(24) I presented my letter to John

Here, the PP *to John* must be analyzed as a complement to *presented*, but given the attachment strategy just sketched, the parser will analyze it as an adjunct to the NP *my letter*. The corresponding structures are given below:

---

[76]Or, in an OV-language like Dutch, a head to its right in the buffer. For ease of exposition we will usually limit ourselves to SVO languages.

(25)

```
(i)        VP                 (ii)       VP
         / | \                          /  \
        V  NP  PP                      V    NP
                                           /  \
                                         NP    PP
```

One potential, though admittedly drastic, way to circumvent this problem is to assume that double object constructions do in fact have the structure (25ii). Then the interpretation of the adjoined PP would be completely dependent upon the θ-marking properties of the verb. This analysis would force us to give up the sisterhood requirement on θ-marking, probably an undesirable result. Still, given an appropriate definition of θ-government, we could maintain that the verb can θ-mark the adjoined PP across an intervening category segment. Observe that this would still be true in a sentence like (26), which would have the structure (27):

(26) I submitted my letter to John to Bill

(27)

```
          VP
         /  \
        V    NP
            /  \
          NP    PP
         /  \
       NP    PP
```

In (27) neither PP is dominated by all NP-segments. This creates an ambiguity problem for θ-marking. How can the parser know which of the two PPs is the verb's complement?

An alternative, and in my view better, approach would be to pop the complete NP off the stack *before* adjunct attachment to check whether or not the head of the node that becomes current next (the VP) requires a PP complement (in addition to an NP complement). Such a strategy would better reflect our intuition that attachment decisions are dependent upon the selectional properties of lexical heads. Suppose we assumed this strategy, then the parser could attach the NP and PP as sisters to the verb, if the verb subcategorized both of these complements. Else the parser would have to push the NP onto the stack again and only then adjoin the PP to the NP. Alternatively, we could assume that the parser attaches the NP as a sister to the verb and adjoins the PP to the VP in such cases, leaving the interpretation of the adjunct to later (semantic) processes.

While these rather sketchy proposals undoubtedly leave many problems untouched, we will not attempt to bring them all to a happy conclusion here. In what follows, we will just pretend that the attachment problems discussed here can be dealt with in one way or another.

The second problem in connection with the adjunction proposal that we have to discuss, concerns our earlier assumption that the number of adjunctions must be strictly finite for the grammar to be parsable by an LRRL(k) parser. This raises an obvious problem with respect to our treatment of overt adjuncts, because an indefinite number of such adjuncts may in fact appear in the input. Now observe that there is an important and, as it turn out, crucial difference between the adjunction of traces and the adjunction of overt adjuncts: while the parser must be able to "remember" the number of adjoined traces in a particular constituent to carry out future parsing decisions (viz. the creation of one or more traces in a new phrase), the parser does not need to "remember" the number of overt adjuncts that it has attached in a particular constituent, simply because that information is not needed for future parsing decisions. As a direct consequence of this, the rules for adjunction of overt adjuncts are finitely representable, and all is well. For additional discussion of this result and an informal proof, see Berwick (1985:pp.315-316).

3.3.3 Licensing the creation of covert categories in A'-position

Summarizing the discussion sofar, we have suggested two extensions of the grammar of the original Marcus parser to accommodate cases of adjunction. Let us now consider the status of these rule packets from the perspective of determinism. Suppose we conceive of the parser as a licensing machine. Its task is to license its input with respect to the grammatical principles that it embodies. On this view, the rule packets that perform adjunctions may be considered a last resort strategy: if the parser is unable to license a particular phrase with respect to the information projected from its lexicon, it performs an ad hoc operation that we might characterize as "stray phrase adjunction". In a very real sense, then, the attachment site of an adjunct is undefined with respect to the grammatical knowledge of the parser.

Now suppose we take advantage of this situation in developing criteria for deterministic chain formation. In particular, suppose we constrain the parser in such a way that it cannot construct a chain link across a node whose attachment site cannot be licensed by grammatical principles. How could we go about doing this? First, suppose we reformulate our definition of antecedent government as follows:

(29) Antecedent Government
α antecedent governs ß iff
(i) the category δ that directly dominates γ, δ and γ not of the same category and γ a maximal category directly dominating ß, does not exclude α,
(ii) α and ß are members of the same chain, and
(iii) no barriers intervene between α and ß

Next, we must define barrierhood. To keep things simple, let us remain neutral about the θ-marking properties of C and I. Instead, we stipulate that the sequence $[_{CP}...[_{IP}...[_{VP}...]]]$ constitutes a Universal Clausal Skeleton (henceforth UCS). By this we mean that the presence of C always implies the presence of IP and that the presence of I always implies the presence of VP[77]. Barrierhood may then be defined as follows:

(30) Barrier
γ is a barrier for α iff γ is neither θ-marked nor implied by the UCS

Next, we assume that the packet A'-ANTECEDENT cannot be activated if the phrase that the parser is about to create constitutes a barrier. The parser can determine barrierhood of the new phrase by (i) consulting the lexical entry of the current head and (ii) by verifying whether or not the new phrase is licensed by the UCS. Finally, we make the further assumption that, if the new phrase is a barrier, the parser activates a packet called NULL-OPERATOR. NULL-OPERATOR creates a null operator and drops it in the first cell of the buffer for subsequent adjunction to the new current. The presence of the null operator will trigger the activation of A'-ANTECEDENT just like any other A'-antecedent. As will become clear later on, these assumptions lead to a unified account of parasitic gaps and certain island violations.

In summary, we tie the distinction between licensed and unlicensed attachment to the creation of A'-traces and null operators, respectively. The corresponding parsing configurations can be characterized as follows. For either the packet A'-ANTECEDENT or NULL-OPERATOR to become active, the current must contain an A'-antecedent. Which of the two packets becomes active is determined by whether or not the phrase that the parser is about to create constitutes a barrier. A phrase is a barrier if it is not θ-marked by the current's head or is not implied by the Universal Clausal Skeleton.

---

[77]Alternatively, we could assume that IP and VP are θ-marked. Nothing of great importance for what follows hinges on the particular choice that we make.

Like the creation of traces, empty operator creation is antecedent dependent, although its antecedent is not necessarily trace. Empty operators have been proposed in the analysis of relative clauses, adjective complements (but not in the *easy to please* construction), purposive-rationale clauses, and more recently for the parasitic gap construction (see Chomsky 1986a). For all of these constructions it can be argued that the clause headed by the null operator is a barrier. The adjective complements that involve empty operator movement are analyzed as in (31):

(31) John$_i$ is too stubborn [O$_i$ [PRO$_k$ to talk to t$_i$]]

For constructions such as these, in which the null operator does not have an A'-antecedent, a separate rule will be required.

There are good reasons to assume that the parasitic gap construction involves empty operator movement as well. Thus, a sentence like (32i) is assigned the S-structure (32ii):

(32) (i) which book did you file without reading
(ii) which book did you file t [O [without [reading e]]]

The evidence for this analysis derives from the observation that the parasitic gap is sensitive to all the standard island effects. The construction is assumed to involve an operation of chain composition, which yields its interpretation (Chomsky 1986a:p.56):

(33) Chain Composition
If $C = (\alpha_1,...,\alpha_n)$ is the chain of the real gap and $C' = (\beta_1,...,\beta_n)$ is the chain of the parasitic gap, then the "composed chain" $(C,C') = (\alpha_1,...,\alpha_n,\beta_1,...,\beta_n)$ is the chain associated with the parasitic gap construction and yields its interpretation.

We can think of chain composition as an interpretive rule that associates the null operator with a category that delimits a range (the overt *wh*-element). Chomsky (op. cit.) assumes that chain composition takes place at S-structure under 0-Subjacency (see section 2.8.1). That is, the real gap and the empty operator must be 0-subjacent at S-structure for chain composition to be possible.

As we have seen, we can integrate the empty operator analysis into our present framework if we tie the distinction between licensed and unlicensed attachment to the activation of the packets A'-ANTECEDENT and NULL-OPERATOR, respectively. This view of the parser's actions implies that the basic parsing engine must come equipped with a set of strategies about what action to take in configurations whose properties cannot be derived from items in the lexicon. Without such strategies, a strictly deterministic parser could not (learn to) parse adjuncts. What drives the insertion of empty operators is a parsing configuration in which the current contains an A'-antecedent and the parser is about to parse a category whose attachment site is linguistically undefined. As a consequence, antecedent government cannot be satisfied and trace insertion is barred.

The reader might wonder whether the "antecedent" for a null operator in parasitic gap constructions should not be a trace in a case-marked θ-position. From the perspective of LRRL(k) parsing this is untenable, however. In the example below the parasitic gap precedes the real gap[78]:

(34) which papers did John decide [before reading e] to tell his secretary [t' [t were unavailable]]

This example shows that the parser must be able to create an empty operator even when it has not yet encountered the real gap. We therefore assume that the parser's ability to create a null operator depends upon the presence of an A'-antecedent in the current.

Finally, we assume that any element (including an empty operator) becomes invisible in the LF-component, unless it has been associated with a referential θ-role or with features that delimit a range. To be precise, we make the following assumptions concerning visibility:

(35) Visibility Condition
 (i) Any element in a chain with a θ-marked position is visible at LF.
 (ii) Any element that delimits a range (i.e. an overt *wh*-element) is visible at LF.

Notice that on these assumption, an empty operator that has been associated with a θ-role is visible at LF. Since we assume, following Chomsky (1986a), that the null operator chain must be licensed at S-structure via Chain Composition, we are committed to the view that Chain Composition applies if and only if the null operator has been associated with a θ-role. To see why, suppose it applied immediately after the creation of the null operator. Then any

[78]A subject trace can only license a parasitic gap that it does not c-command. We will suggest an explanation for this peculiarity later on.

null operator would automatically be associated with a category that delimits a range and hence be visible at LF. In cases in which the null operator does not bind a trace in a θ-position, this would give rise to a violation of the Bijection Principle. We therefore assume that Chain Composition is a rule that applies to the output of the parser in the mapping to LF.

With things set up this way, we allow the parser to hypothesize the existence of a parasitic gap and be wrong. For if it is wrong, the null operator will not be linked to a θ-role and Chain Composition will not apply, rendering the empty operator invisible at LF.

3.3.4 The form and interpretation of adjunct-operator chains

It follows from the assumptions we have made sofar that the best the parser will ever do for an adjunct-operator like *why* is build a maximal chain of adjoined traces. Because adjuncts are not projected from the lexicon, there can be no traces of adjuncts in non-adjoined positions. In particular, let us assume that the foot of an adjunct-operator chain is a VP-adjoined position and that adjunct-operator chains are interpreted at LF. The interpretation of such chains presumably involves selecting one of the VP-adjoined traces in the chain as the foot of the chain and construing the adjunct with this VP.

One way to execute this idea would be to follow a proposal of Rizzi (1988), who essentially follows Chomsky (1981), and assumes a fundamental split between arguments, which are referential expressions potentially referring to participants in an event, and quasi-arguments, which are expressions that carry a θ-role but do not refer to a participant, such as the subjects of weather verbs and the nominal parts of idioms. "We can thus distinguish between argumental or referential θ-roles (agent, theme, patient, experiencer, goal, etc.) and quasi-argumental or non-referential θ-roles (manner, measure, atmospheric role, idiosyncratic role in idioms, etc.)" (Rizzi,pp.13-14). We could then assume that referential θ-roles are associated with lexical items via the lexicon, as described above, and that non-referential θ-roles are not assigned but are an inherent property of what we call adjuncts. On this view, adjunct-operators, too, would have an inherent θ-role and their interpretation, which we assume takes place at LF, would involve calculating its launching site from the chain built by the parser. There are good reasons for the further assumption that the interpretation of such chains is left-to-right, because the adjunct must be construed with the first candidate VP in a left-to-right scan, unless the verb heading the VP happens to be a so-called parenthetical like *say* or *think*[79].

With this analysis of adjunct-operators in mind, consider once more the data that we discussed earlier as 3.2.3 (9) and (10):

(36) (i) ? what$_i$ did [t$_i$ [you [t$_i$ [wonder [$_{CP}$t$_i$ [$_{IP}$t$_i$ [$_{IP}$ [to whom]$_k$ to [t$_k$ [t$_i$ [PRO give t$_i$ t$_k$]]]]]]]]]]]

(ii) * how$_j$ do [t$_j$ [you [t$_j$ [wonder [t$_j$ [what$_i$ to [t$_j$ [t$_i$ [PRO repair t$_i$ t$_j$]]]]]]]]

In section 3.2.3 we suggested that *to whom* in (36i) and *what* in (36ii) would have to move to specCP at LF. In both cases that movement would destroy a chain link of the chain formed by the *wh*-element in the upstairs clause. However, in (36i) the lower half of the broken chain remains visible at LF, because its foot is a θ-marked trace. In (36ii), by contrast, the lower chain does not contain a θ-marked position and therefore cannot escape invisibility at LF (cf. the Visibility Condition (35)). On these assumptions, the relative acceptability of (36i) may be attributed to the existence of a well-formed chain at LF. The rigid unacceptability of (36i) under the intended reading (an ECP violation in the competence grammar) results from the invisibility of the lower chain half.

3.3.5 Why the insertion of empty operators must be antecedent-dependent

Berwick and Weinberg (1985a) argue on the basis of rather different assumptions about visibility that the insertion of empty operators need not be cued to the presence of an antecedent for the empty operator. By their version of visibility, the chain headed by the empty operator will not be visible in the Propositional Node Stack (the semantic component of their parsing model), unless it is associated with (i) a θ-role *and* (ii) a c-commanding category that delimits a range (i.e. an overt *wh*-operator) or an individual[80]. By these criteria a bound anaphor (which is an element with no intrinsic semantic features) would not be visible in the PNS unless it was bound by a c-commanding antecedent denoting an individual.

---

[79]A very similar approach to θ-role assignment to adjuncts was sketched by Jean-Roger Vergnaud in a talk held at the 1988 LF-conference in Tilburg. He also pointed out that the class of parentheticals is much smaller than the class of bridge verbs.

[80]Whereas in our Visibility Condition these two requirements are disjunctive with respect to each other, they must be conjunctively satisfied in Berwick and Weinberg's condition.

(37) Visibility Condition (Berwick and Weinberg 1985a:p.28)
To be visible in the PNS, an element must be associated with a θ-role (either by occupying a θ-position or binding an element in a θ-position) and must have referential features (features that either designate an individual or set of individuals or that delimit a range).

According to Berwick and Weinberg, these conditions on visibility allow the parser to create an empty operator at the beginning of any adjunct phrase, independently of the presence of an antecedent. They give the examples below to make their case:

(38) (i) who_i did you meet e_i without [OP_j [$_{IP}$ greeting e_j]]
(ii) did you watch the movie without [OP_j [$_{IP}$ eating e_j]]

In (38i) there is an overt operator that delimits a range with which the empty operator can be associated. The null operator also binds an element in a θ-position, so all is well: the null operator chain can be interpreted at LF and (38i) gets a parasitic gap reading. In (38ii) the empty operator cannot be linked to a category that delimits a range and therefore the chain headed by the empty operator becomes invisible in the PNS, as required.

They go on to remark that:

> ". . . this solution will only work for *empty* operators. Lexically specified elements will receive a phonetic interpretation but no semantic interpretation, a situation that will lead to unacceptability." (p.29)

This cannot be correct, however. The dummy subjects *it* and *there* receive a phonetic but no semantic interpretation with a perfectly acceptable result. In fact, this is just what one would expect if the LF and PF branches of the grammar are completely blind to each other's operations, which would seem to be the only reasonable position anyway. This, then, leads to the first serious problem with this approach to empty operators: there is no way to exclude violations of the Bijection Principle, because the guilty party is invisible at LF. Thus, (39) is predicted to be fine:

(39) * who John kisses Mary

Next, Berwick and Weinberg remark that "the astute reader will have noted an apparent problem created by this solution". The problem is that, since empty elements can become invisible at later stages, there seems to be no motivation to cue their creation to the presence of an antecedent. Take a verb like *eat*, which can be either transitive or intransitive. The parser could always assume that *eat* was transitive, because if it turned out that there was no antecedent for the object trace, then it would simply become invisible. Hence, it would seem that the approach to parasitic gaps undermines their functional account of Subjacency. The solution to this apparent problem, the authors argue, lies in the fact that

> ". . . it is only elements with no phonetic features that can escape unacceptability if they are not semantically interpreted. Since *wh*-elements have case features, they will be visible in the phonological component."
> (p.30)

Again Berwick and Weinberg seem to suggest that PF and LF each know what the other is doing. But apart from that, they must be overlooking a contradiction in their argument. If the variable in (40i) below is visible at PF then so is the variable in (38ii), repeated here as (40ii):

(40) (i) did you think Fred had eaten e_j
(ii) did you watch the movie without [OP_j [$_s$ eating e_j]]

Therefore, we would expect (40ii) to be ruled out on exactly the same grounds as (40i), which again suggests that the creation of a null operator must be licensed by an antecedent.

3.3.6 Extraction from adjuncts and adjunct parasitic gaps

Let us now consider how the proposed parsing model accounts for the Adjunct Condition. Consider the data below:

(41) (i) * to whom did they leave [before speaking t]
(ii) * who did they leave [before speaking to t]
(iii) * why did they leave [before speaking to John t]
(iv) ok what did you file t [without reading e]

Let us go through each of these examples in turn. In (41i,ii) the parser will adjoin traces to all maximal projections dominating the adjunct. At this point in the parse antecedent government is blocked, because the parser cannot license the attachment site of the adjunct. It therefore activates the packet NULL-OPERATOR. After the null operator has been created and attached to the adjunct, the parser constructs a chain terminating in a θ-position[81]. Hence, Chain Composition will apply in the mapping to LF, making the empty operator chains visible at LF. Omitting irrelevant details, the parser's output for these sentences is as in (42):

(42) $[_{CP}(\text{to})\ wh_i ... [_{IP} t_i ... [[_{VP} t_i ...]]]$
$[_{PP} O_j ... [_{CP} t_j ... [_{IP} t_j ... [_{VP} t_j .. V t_j]]]]]$

We see then that the parser's counterpart of a strong Subjacency violation (2-subjacent movement in the Barriers theory) is a parasitic structure without a true gap. We discuss the implications of this result with respect to the Bijection Principle in the following section.

The contrast between (41i,ii) and (41iii), which is much worse, we attribute, as before, to a complete failure to construct a null operator chain in the adjunct that is visible at LF. Finally, (41iv) receives a fine parasitic gap analysis.

We conclude that the parser explains the Adjunct Condition in the sense that the packet activation scheme that is responsible for the account is grounded in the opposition between licensed and unlicensed attachment. There is simply no way in which a strictly deterministic parser can determine that the attachment site of an adjunct will be validated by later parsing processes, for instance at LF. Because attachment decisions that are based upon ad hoc strategies are undefined with respect to the grammar that the parser incorporates, no linguistics predicates (such as c-command and government) can be computed by the parser over the structures that are the result of such decisions. In fact, this is what drives the insertion of empty operators: null operators are inserted in environments in which the current contains an A'-antecedent and the parser is about to parse a category whose attachment site is grammatically undefined. As a consequence, antecedent government cannot be satisfied and trace insertion is barred.

It should be noted that, while exactly the same result might be argued to hold for a backtracking parser, this would not be the case for a parser that can output more than one analysis in parallel. Such a parser could produce parallel analyses, representing all possible attachment sites for an adjunct. It could therefore safely posit a trace at the beginning of an adjunct, because all

[81]We will discuss an additional constraint on the creation of traces in A-positions later on, but that will leave the present account untouched.

representations with invalid adjunct attachments could be destroyed in the LF-component.

3.3.7 Extraction from subjects and subject parasitic gaps

The above account of extraction from adjuncts can be extended to account for the ungrammaticality of extraction from subjects. Consider the data that we have to account for:

(43) (i) * I wonder who$_i$ [$_{NP}$a picture of t$_i$] is on sale
(ii) ? I wonder who$_i$ [$_{NP}$a picture of e$_i$] surprised t$_i$
(iii) * I wonder [why$_i$ [[[$_{VP}$t$_i$ [$_{VP}$ reading the book]]]] would be fun]

As we have seen in the case of adjuncts the simple fact that the parser incorporates a rule for attaching a phrase does not in and of itself guarantee that that phrase is not a barrier for antecedent government. In particular, a phrase that is neither θ-marked nor implied by the UCS is a barrier for antecedent government. Now suppose we assume, as before, that specIP is a θ-bar position, and that subjects are assigned a θ-role in specVP. Then a phrase in specIP will be a barrier for antecedent government, as will be required to account for the facts in (43). It follows that the embedded clause in (43i) will be assigned the structure (44) below (irrelevant details omitted):

(44) * I wonder [$_{CP}$who$_i$ [$_{IP}$t$_i$ [$_{NP}$O$_j$ [$_{NP}$ a picture [$_{PP}$t$_j$ [$_{PP}$ of t$_j$]]]] is on sale]]

So again the parser's counterpart of a strong Subjacency violations turns out to be a defective parasitic gap structure. For (43ii), the parser outputs a fine parasitice gap structure, while we attribute the complete ungrammaticality of (43iii) under the intended reading to a complete failure to construct a visible null-operator chain.

Let us assume that chains are subject to the following well-formedness conditions:

(45) Chain Condition (LF)
A maximal A-chain ($\alpha_1,...,\alpha_n$) has exactly one Case-marked position (namely, α_1) and exactly one θ-marked position (namely, α_n).
(Chomsky 1986a:p.63)

(46) Bijection Principle (LF)
An operator binds exactly one variable.
(Koopman and Sportiche 1982)

The chains in (42) and (44) violate the Bijection Principle. It would seem that one would like to say a little bit more about these cases than just that, however. For although (42) and (44) violate this principle, they are certainly not as unintelligible as (47):

(47) I wonder who John bought the book

This suggests that (42) and (44) may be subject to some sort of "repair procedure" in the mapping to LF that can do nothing to improve (47). There is one very conspicuous property of empty operators that sets them apart from their overt counterparts: indexation. By the Visibility Condition, an empty operator can and should be coindexed with an overt operator, whereas overt operators may never be coindexed with another overt operator. It seems likely that it is this property of empty operators that mitigates violations of the Bijection Principle of the sort in (42) and (44). Let us make this intuition explicit:

(48) Chain Optimization
If a composed chain violates the Bijection Principle, reinterpret the null operator as trace.

Chain Optimization is not intended as a principle of grammar, but as a "toolkit" interpretation rule that is only invoked after the damage has been done. I suggest that such toolkit rules enable people to come up with an interpretation for sentences that we know violate one or more linguistic principles.

3.3.8 Extraction from objects and the non-existence of object parasitic gaps

Extraction from θ-marked complements is generally possible, but subject to a specificity constraint that we will not discuss here:

(49) (i) ok who did you see $[_{NP}$t $[_{NP}$a picture of t]
(ii) ok who did John say $[_{CP}$t that he had seen t]
(iii) ok why did John say $[_{CP}$t that he had $[_{VP}$t $[_{VP}$ married Susan]]]
(iv) * who_i did John promise t_i [t_i that he would see e_i]

Because the object is θ-marked, antecedent government into the object is not blocked and trace insertion is possible, while empty operator insertion is barred[82]. This means that in (49iv) the empty element in the embedded specCP must be trace and cannot be an empty operator (but see section 3.3.10). Therefore, the resulting structure violates the Bijection Principle. The simple generalization that we arrive at is that there can only be a parasitic gap within a constituent that is a barrier to syntactic movement (but see the previous footnote).

3.3.9 Licensing the creation of traces in A-positions

Sofar the only constraint upon trace creation that we have discussed is the Condition on Chain Links: a trace must be antecedent governed. However, if our proposal is to be reasonably empirically adequate, we will have to impose an additional constraint on the creation of (at least some) traces in A-positions. Consider the following cases of *wh*-movement from subject position:

(50) (i) ok who do you think t left
(ii) * who do you think that t left
(iii) ok wie denk je dat t vertrok
who think you that left
who do you think that left

At the point at which the parser has analyzed the matrix verb in these sentences, it is in the configuration below:

[82]This account abstracts away from instances of parasitic gaps that appear to be incompatible with the anti-c-command requirement, such as the example below (cf. Engdahl 1984 and Hudson 1984):

ok which men did the police warn t [that they were about to arrest e]

Similarly, many Dutch informants claim a parasitic gap reading for the Dutch equivalent of (49iv). In order to account for these facts within the present framework, one would have to assume that for these informants the second object is in fact an adjunct, which seems incorrect. My own judgement of the Dutch data is that the parasitic gap reading is only present if the embedded clause is infinitival:

ok Wie heb je beloofd t [e van de trein te zullen halen]
who did you promise t [to to pick up e at the station]
* Wie heb je beloofd t [dat je e van de trein zult halen]
who did you promise t [that you would pick up e at the station]

We leave this problem unsolved.

(51) *Stack (3 deep)*

1 CP
      SPEC:(who_i/wie_i)
      C:($do_k/denk_m$)
2 IP
      t_i
      IP
        NP:(you_p/je_p)
        I'
          I:(t_k/t_m)
3 VP
      t_i
      VP
        SPEC:(t_p)
        V'
          V:(think/t_m)

Buffer

1 V:(left/vertrok)
2 #:(.)
3

Unseen Words

None.

No active rule packets have been indicated in (51), but the packets associated with the VP at least include PARSE-VP and A'-ANTECEDENT. As the verb *think/denken* subcategorizes a CP, a new CP is pushed on the stack, and the packets PARSE-CP and A'-ANTECEDENT are activated for the construction of this node. After a trace has been created and attached (and, in 50ii and 50iii, the complementizer has been attached), the parser creates the IP and activates the packets PARSE-IP and A'-ANTECEDENT for its construction. Next, a trace is created and adjoined to IP. If at this point in the parse the CCL were the only constraint governing the creation of the trace in specIP, we would expect (50i,ii,iii) to be all grammatical. When the gap in the IP is detected, the current contains an antecedent and everything should be well. In the Barriers framework the ungrammaticality of (50ii) is accounted for by the Minimality Condition, which states that antecedent government is blocked by an intervening governor. In (50ii) the complementizer *that* induces a violation of the Minimality Condition. For some obscure reason the Dutch complementizer *dat* does not give rise to a violation of this condition. Here we will try to account for the facts without taking recourse to the Minimality Condition.

First observe that if we abstract from the selectional properties of the matrix verbs in (50i-iii), the parse of each of these sentences is locally ambiguous. The specifier could be either trace or PRO. There are in fact cases in which the selecting verb would not resolve the ambiguity:

(52) (i) who did John claim PRO to have seen t
(ii) who did John claim t had seen the accident

This implies that there are cases in which the parser's decision to insert trace or PRO is fully dependent upon case-marking. Suppose, therefore, that in such cases the parser relies on information about case-marking only to decide whether to insert trace or PRO. The obvious suggestion would seem to be that the parser must consult its buffer to see whether the verb that follows is tensed. Unfortunately, this is a catch 22, as there are cases in which such a test will fail:

(53) who did John believe t to have left

In cases of exceptional case-marking, the parser must rely on properties of the matrix verb to make a decision about the content of the specifier of IP. Now consider how the parser could have access to this information when it parses the IP. If only the current is accessible to parsing rules, then information about case-marking properties of the governing verb will not be available when the parser is constructing the IP, because the VP is no longer current at this point. How can this problem be solved? Suppose exceptional case-marking takes place under a parsing analogue of SPEC-head agreement. Specifically, assume that *believe* assigns a case-feature to the IP at the moment of its creation and that this case-feature may be transferred to the specifier of IP after the specifier has been attached. Then, in the most difficult case that is possible (trace insertion in an exceptional case-marking environment) the only reliable source of information for the parser will be the absence or presence of a case-feature on the IP. We assume that case-marking takes place under a parsing analogue of government.

Returning now to the examples that set off this discussion (50i-iii), suppose we generalize the approach just sketched and assume that in these cases, too, the IP must be marked for case for trace insertion to be licit. In addition, let us stick to the idea that the case-feature must be assigned under government. Then, the only way to case-mark the IP in (50i-iii) is by inserting an AGR-element in the head of CP. For this to work properly, the insertion of AGR must be dependent upon the presence of a tensed verb in the buffer. While these assumptions lead to a good account of the facts, it should be noted that we cannot show their *necessity*.

The data in (50) can now be accounted for as follows. Suppose that in English insertion of AGR in C is impossible if C contains the complementizer *that*, while in Dutch the complementizer *dat* contains AGR-features. These assumptions will be motivated below.

Finally, notice that since no parsing ambiguity occurs if the specifier of IP is a full NP (i.e. if it is part of the input), no case-feature need appear on IP. In those cases, the NP is assigned case by the head of IP (either under government or under SPEC-head agreement in the sense of Chomsky 1986a).

We will develop the AGR-insertion idea along the lines of an idea that has surfaced in the works of several authors (cf. e.g. Chomsky 1981, Pesetsky 1981). Here we discuss a proposal by Rizzi (1987), who discusses AGR-insertion in C for reasons quite similar to ours. In particular, Rizzi assumes a conjunctive version of the ECP that requires traces to be simultaneously antecedent governed and head governed[83]. This raises rather obvious problems with respect to movement from subject position in cases like (50i-iii). Rizzi suggests that SPEC-head agreement is an agreement relation between a phrase in the specifier and an agreement element in the head and that in English a tensed complementizer can be realized as *that* or AGR:

(54) C → AGR/that

Rizzi notes that "these options are in complementary distribution in standard English (but not in some dialects)". Further, the expansion (54) is optional, while, "in general, an occurrence of AGR must be licensed by coindexation with its specifier" (p.24). Under these assumptions, (55i) has the structure (55ii), (56i) the structure (56ii) and (57i) the structure (57ii):

(55) (i) ok who do you think left
(ii) who_i do [t_i [you [t_i [think [t_i AGR_i [t_i left]]]]]]
(56) (i) * who do you that think left
(ii) who_i do [t_i [you [t_i [think [t_i that [t_i left]]]]]]
(57) (i) ok who left
(ii) who_i AGR_i t_i left

Rizzi assumes that that it is the AGR element that head governs the trace in

[83]Rizzi requires a head governor to be lexical, where A, N, A, P, and AGR are lexical.

subject position.

Similar phenomena requiring a parallel analysis can be found in many languages. Perhaps the best-known example is the *que*-to-*qui* rule in French (irrelevant details omitted):

(58) (i) * l'homme que je crois t que t viendra
the man that I believe that will come
(ii) ok l'homme que je crois t qui t viendra
the man that I believe will come

Interestingly, the *que*-to-*qui* rule is blocked in the case of object extraction (59) and in the case of extraction of an embedded subject (60):

(59) (i) ok l'homme que je crois t que Jean connait t
the man that I believe that John knows
(ii) * l'homme que je crois t qui Jean connait t
the man that I believe that John knows
(60) (i) ok l'homme que je pense t que Jean croit t qui t viendra
(ii) * l'homme que je pense t qui Jean croit t qui t viendra
the man that I think John believes will come

Rizzi assumes that for French *qui* is *que*+ARG and that for some unknown reason the AGR-element in C must be indentical to (coindexed with) the AGR-element in I[84]. Of course, we have no way of knowing if the same holds true of Dutch, because there is no overt agreement on the complementizer. But West-Flemish has a *dat*-to-*die* rule that is quite comparable to the French *que*-to-*qui* rule (Goeman 1980, Bennis & Haegeman 1983, Haegeman 1983). Frisian shows (defective) complementizer agreement as well. In that language second person singular is spelled out on the complementizer (Hoekstra and Marácz 1989). And as in French, the agreement element in C and I must be identical. Bavarian has a similar rule as well (Bayer 1984).

Rizzi also discusses two languages, Kinande, a Bantu language spoken in north eastern Zaire, and Modern Irish, which show SPEC-head agreement in CP without the requirement that C and I have identical agreement. See Rizzi (op. cit.) for particulars.

Let us now compare our AGR-insertion proposal to Rizzi's. Unlike Rizzi, we have no reason to assume that the government requirement that must be met by a trace in specIP must be met by all traces. On our view a trace in specIP

[84]One might of course speculate that languages like French just do not have an object agreement element.

must sometimes meet a case-government requirement to avoid a parsing ambiguity. The insertion site for traces itself is never ambiguous. If a gap is detected and trace insertion (i.e. creation and attachment) is possible, then trace insertion is obligatory. By contrast, if an unambiguous gap is detected and trace insertion is impossible, then insertion of either PRO or pro must be possible. If no empty category can be licensed for an unambiguous gap, the parser goes into an error condition.

3.3.10 Why parasitic gaps cannot be licensed by a wh-trace in subject position

As is well known, a parasitic gap cannot be licensed by a c-commanding variable. A typical example appears below:

(61) * who [t [spoke to you [before [O [you met e]]]]]

As has been noted by Longobardi (1988) the restriction is not just that subjects cannot license a parasitic gap but must be stated in terms of c-command:

(62) (i) * a man who [t looks old [whenever I meet e]]
(ii) ? a man who [whenever I meet] [t looks old]

As pointed out by Chomsky (1986a), who cites the example below due to Andrew Barrs, a subject trace can regularly license a parasitic gap if it is more deeply embedded than the parasitic gap:

(63) (i) ok which paper did John decide [before reading e] to tell his secretary [t' [t were unavailable]]
(ii) * which papers [t were unavailable [before you discovered e]]

It would seem that the approach to chain formation that we have developed in this chapter allows a natural explanation of these facts. As we have seen the parser can postulate a null operator and be wrong, because the null operator becomes invisible if it cannot be linked to a θ-role. Now consider the configuration the parser will be in after having created the subject trace in (63ii):

(64) *Stack*

1 CP

SPEC:(which papers$_i$)

C:(AGR$_i$)

2 IP

t_i

IP

t_i

I'

I_i:(past)

Because the parser has inserted a trace in an A-position, it must now create the VP and activate the packets PARSE-VP and A-ANTECEDENT. Notice that we cannot assume that it also activates A'-ANTECEDENT, because that would give rise to illegal chains such as the one below:

(65) Who$_i$ t_i kissed t_i

In other words, the parser cannot create the A'-trace and be wrong (as was the case with null operator creation), because it cannot be sure that the gap it eventually finds will be inside a phrase that is a barrier and hence bound by a null operator.

The parse continues in a straightforward manner. Once the gap in specVP has been detected, a trace is created and inserted in this position. Next, an AP is created with the active packets PARSE-AP and A-ANTECEDENT. Then a trace is created and inserted in specAP. Because the θ-marked foot of the chain has been found and the AP does not contain an A'-antecedent, none of the packets A'-ANTECEDENT, A-ANTECEDENT or NULL-OPERATOR can be activated upon creation of the adjunct[85]. Hence, the parser will declare an error when it detects the unambiguous gap in the adjunct, because it cannot license the creation of an empty category as the complement of *discovered*. Similarly, the parser will declare an error in (62i), because it cannot license the creation of an empty category as the complement of *meet*. Sentences like (62i) and (63ii) should therefore have the extremely degraded status of (66), which is correct:

(66) * John bought

[85]Notice that we cannot assume that the caseless trace in specAP is a proper antecedent for empty-operator creation.

Chomsky notes that :

> "the failure of c-commanding subjects to license parasitic gaps . . . is a far stronger effect than Subjacency. In fact, it has the extreme character of a government violation of the ECP variety". (Chomsky 1986a:p.65)

Under our analysis this comes as no surprise: the extreme ungrammaticality results from the absence of an antecedent governor for the detected unambiguous gap. In cases like (62ii,63i) the creation of the null operator *precedes* the creation of the A-trace and all is well.

3.4 Summary of results

In this chapter we have developed an informal extension to the runtime grammar of the Marcus parser that handles the creation and attachment of empty categories, and the attachment of adjuncts. It was shown that a Marcus parser that does not use feature annotations for encoding the presence of an antecedent enforces a very strong locality constraint on traces of syntactic movement, the Condition on Chain Links (CCL), which we defined in terms of a restrictive definition of antecedent government. This version of the CCL accounts for the unacceptability of super-raising and super-passive, and of violations of the *Wh*-Island Condition in quite similar ways. What is the status of the functional explantion of the CCL in terms of Fodor's classification of types of functional explanation, discussed in section 1.5.1? Of course, the functional account is at least type 1: i.e. the parser can be made to obey the CCL. However, a good case can be made for regarding the account as type 3, because the CCL is implied by the defining properties of the parser, on the assumption that the parser does not use features that are unmotivated from the point of view of the grammar that the parser implements. As it is reasonable to maintain that the use of features annotations must be empirically motivated, the minimal assumption is that the Marcus parser does not use such features.

In section 3.2.4 we established the important result that unrestricted adjunction does affect grammar size in a way that could give rise to computational intractability.

In section 3.3 we argued that the islandhood of adjuncts and subjects can be made to follow from the property of determinism in the sense that a deterministic parser that computes an S-structure cannot license the attachment site of adjuncts and subjects with respect to grammatical principles. By contrast, a parser that can build representations in parallel computes all possible attachment sites of an adjunct. All resulting analyses are then input to an LF-parser, which can destroy all representations for which it cannot validate the attachment site of an adjunct. The functional account of the Adjunct Condition and the Subject Condition is at least type 1, because the Marcus parser can be made to obey these conditions. However, it is arguably type 3, because the fact that the attachment sites of adjunct and subjects cannot be licensed is not at all arbitrary with respect to the Marcus parser, but may be said to be entailed by the (limited) grammatical knowledge to which it has access. In particular, the defining properties that give rise to the functional account are its inability to compute parallel analyses and the fact that it does not have access to properties of LF.

It was also shown that the proposed parsing model can be made to obey the *that*-trace filter. Because we could not show the necessity of the assumptions that give rise to this behavior, the functional account of the *that*-trace filter is only type 1.

Finally, the parser provides a type 3 explanation for the non-existence of parasitic gaps that are c-commanded by a trace in subject position. This explanation was based on the demonstration that the parser cannot create an A'-trace and be wrong, without desastrous effects. This in sharp contrast with null operator creation.

Chapter 4

Epilogue

4.1 Summary

The central aim of my investigation has been to clarify the (possible) relations between competence theories and algorithmic theories, and, in particular, between competence grammars and their corresponding parsers. In chapter one I addressed the notion of grammar-parser relation from a broad cognitive view, arguing that there are no a priori reasons to expect a very tight relation between the grammar and the parser that realizes it. There are no reasons to expect different conclusions would be appropriate in other cognitive domains.

It is quite conceivable that future investigations into these matters will have to deal with far more unsettling discrepancies between the levels of the Computational Framework than the ones we have addressed. In particular, I believe that, if the rapidly developing field of connectionism, in which various attempts have been made to model various cognitive abilities in terms of neural networks, turns out to be a fruitful avenue, many new and intriguing questions will have to be asked about the role of competence theories in the development of algorithmic theories. At present the conceptual abyss between the two fields is so enormous that it is hard to characterize a relation between cognitive theories and their corresponding neural model at all. Part of the problem seems to be that cognitive theorists think in terms of symbol manipulation, which in turn reflects the sound scientific attitude that the very complex problems humans deal with almost effortlessly should have a well-structured solution. The neural networks that have been developed to model certain human cognitive abilities are best viewed as machines that do non-symbolic processing. In addition, while (some of) these networks do their work very well indeed, it is usually hard to see why. The network does not in any sense seem to embed a well-structured solution to the problem that it was designed to solve. Although this state of affairs might be partly due to the current level of understanding in the field of neural networks, the two approaches sketched here are of a qualitatively very different nature and reconciling them will undoubtedly turn out to be a difficult if not elusive task.

Chapter one also took up the characterization of the concept of psychological reality. What does it mean to say that a grammar is psychologically real? Drawing on work by Abney (1988), we sketched six grammar-parser relations, each of which imposed different constraints on the ways the grammar and the parser could be different from each other.

I then presented a short historical survey of the most important developments in grammatical theorizing and natural language processing following the failure of the Derivational Theory of Complexity. Here, as in most of the book, I disregarded much interesting work in automatic translation and other areas of application, choosing instead to focus on those developments that seemed most relevant to the cognition-oriented line of discussion.

Finally, drawing on work by Fodor (1985), I showed how the concept of functional explanation is intimately connected with the relation grammar-parser. I then reviewed Fodor's three types of explanation, which range from mere incorporation of a grammatical constraint C by a parser P to true explanation of C by P. I reinterpreted Fodor's *Type 1* functional account as a minimal grammar-parser correspondence. The point here was that, if the function computed by P is a superset of the function specified by the grammar for which P is (supposed to be) a parser, and P cannot be appropriately restricted to remedy this shortcoming, then P is simply not a parser for that grammar. I also pointed out some of the complexities involved in giving an efficiency (*Type 2*) or a strategy (*Type 3*) argument for the existence of a linguistic constraint.

In chapter two we first gave an outline of the Marcus parser, which was followed by a critical discussion of some arguments against its lookahead buffer. In section 2.6 I gave an overview of Nozohoor-Farshi's (1986) formal characterization of the Marcus parser. It was concluded that the Marcus parser is a restricted LRRL(k) parser and not a Bounded Context or LR(k) parser, as has been claimed by Berwick and Weinberg (1984) & Berwick (1985). In section 2.7 we embarked upon a detailed study of the functional explanation of Subjacency of Berwick and Weinberg (1984) and showed that their conclusions were overly optimistic. It turned out that the most that can be derived from their modified Marcus parser is the *Wh*-Island Condition. I also argued against Berwick and Weinberg's (op. cit.) conclusion that there is no functional derivation in terms of a parser of a Subjacency-like constraint for a GPSG framework, and showed that the same modified Marcus parser would suffice to account for the existence of the *S/α,ß-filter of Chung and McCloskey (1983). Finally, I gave a summary of my own (1987) paper, in which I attempted to show that the Marcus parser explains (parts of) the Subjacency constraint as reformulated in *Barriers* (Chomsky, 1986a), and pointed out several deficiencies of that proposal. I ended the chapter with an upbeat promise, claiming that some of the key ideas of my paper might be fruitfully incorporated in a deterministic parsing model that incorporated a specific implementation of the concept of *attachment decision*.

Even more than chapter two, chapter three was a case study of a particular grammar-parser relation. The idea I had in mind was to fix a number of properties of the parser and to deduce from this constrained parser certain properties of natural languages. What were these properties? First, I assumed that Berwick and Weinberg's no-counting argument was valid: i.e. grammars cannot count (origin of property: the grammatical theory). Second, I assumed that the parser does not use any features that are unmotivated from the point of view of the grammar that it embeds (origin of property: a particular assumption (in fact, the minimal one) about grammar-parser equivalence). Third, I assumed that the parser is deterministic and, more specifically, that it is a (restricted) LRRL(k) parser (origin of property: parsing theory).

It had already been shown in chapter two that the first and third of these assumptions suffice to account for the existence of the *Wh*-Island Condition. In section 3.2 I showed that a stronger result is obtained if the second assumption is included in the model as well: in that case the parser cannot analyze instances of super-raising and super-passive either.

Then, in section 3.3, I developed a chain algorithm that crucially relies on the distinction between licensed and unlicensed attachment, which in turn is directly dependent upon the property of strict determinism. I then argued that the proposed chain algorithm, in conjunction with certain assumptions about chain visibility, explains the existence of the Subject Condition and the Adjunct Condition.

4.2 Conclusions: The Relation Grammar-Parser Revisited

There are several aspects of the analysis proposed in chapter three that merit further discussion, because of their potential implications for the competence theory we assumed, i.e. the Barriers theory.

Perhaps the most striking characteristic of the parser's behavior is that it gives rise to outputs that are not always identical to the structures generated by the grammar. As a typical example, compare the S-structure generated by the grammar (1ii) to the output of the parser (1iii) for a sentence that violates the Adjunct Condition:

(1) (i) * who did you go to London without consulting
(ii) $[_{CP}$who$_i$ did $[_{IP}$you $[_{VP}$t$_i$ $[_{VP}$go]] $[_{PP}$to London] $[_{PP}$t$_i$ $[_{PP}$without $[_{CP}$t$_i$ $[_{IP}$PRO $[_{VP}$t$_i$ $[_{VP}$consulting t$_i$]]]]]]]]

(iii) $[_{CP}$who$_i$ did $[_{IP}t_i$ $[_{IP}[_{IP}[_{IP}$you $[_{VP}t_i$ $[_{VP}$go] $[_{PP}$to London] $[_{PP}O_i$ $[_{PP}$without $[_{CP}t_i$ $[_{IP}$PRO $[_{VP}t_i$ $[_{VP}$consulting t_i]]]]]]]]]]]

Let us first discuss (1ii) in some more detail. According to the analysis Chomsky finally settles on in *Barriers*, *who* adjoines to the adjunct PP before moving on to adjoin to the matrix VP. He is committed to this analysis, because he must assume that in an analogous parasitic gap structure the null operator adjoins to the adjunct PP to satisfy the 0-Subjacency requirement on Chain Composition. In other words the structure for (2i) must be (2ii) and not (2iii) (irrelevant details omitted):

(2) (i) which book did you file without reading
(ii) which book did you file t [O[without reading t]]
(iii) which book did you file t without [O reading t]]

However, once adjunction to adjunct PPs is allowed, a new problem arises. As adjunction voids barrierhood, we would expect movement out of adjuncts to be generally possible. Chomsky gives the following examples to substantiate the claim that this prediction is essentially correct (Chomsky's (63)):

(3) (i) * He is the person to whom $[_{IP}$they left [before speaking t]]
(ii) ? He is the person who $[_{IP}$they left [before speaking to t]] (before meeting t)

As (3ii) is fairly acceptable, the problem under this new analysis would seem to be the unacceptability of (3i). To account for these facts, he then stipulates that only NP is permitted to adjoin to the PP adjunct position. This would then also explain the rigid unacceptability of adjunct extraction from adjunct PPs:

(4) * how did you leave [before fixing the car]

Contrary to what Chomsky claims, however, the facts in (3) do not at all suggest that extraction from adjuncts is (relatively) acceptable for NPs. The acceptability of (3ii) is simply due to the fact that it admits the parasitic gap reading (5):

(5) ? He is the person who $[_{IP}$they left t [O [before speaking to e]] (O before meeting e)

For (3i), by contrast, there is no parasitic reading because *leave* does not take a PP complement. This interpretation of the facts is confirmed by (6i,ii) below. In (6i) the matrix verb is intransitive, while in (6ii) the matrix verb is transitive but no movement has applied to its complement. In either case extraction out of the adjunct leads to rigid unacceptability:

(6) (i) * He is the person who [$_{IP}$they slept [O [before speaking to e]] (O before meeting e)
(ii) * He is the person who [$_{IP}$they left Bill [O [before speaking to e]] (O before meeting e)

We conclude that Chomsky's suggestion that extraction out of adjuncts yields acceptable results for NPs is incorrect. This leads to a rather serious problem for the Barriers theory. If adjunction to adjuncts must be allowed for null operators, there seems to be no way to get adjuncts to behave as barriers with respect to extraction. In particular, it seems quite impossible to account for the observations in terms of a theory of adjunction.

The parsing account of the adjunct condition does not rely on ad hoc assumptions about adjunction at all. By contrast, we have taken the view that adjunction is always allowed (though not more than once to the same maximal projection). Instead, the parser's behaviour is a result of the interplay of five key assumptions: (i) the parser is deterministic, (ii) θ-marking licenses attachment, (iii) structural relations (such as c-command and government) cannot be computed over unlicensed tree fragments, (iv) if the current contains an A'-antecedent and the requirement of antecedent government cannot be met, the parser creates a null operator, and (v) any element in a chain with a θ-marked position is visible at LF and so is any element that delimits a range (our Visibility Condition, cf. 3.3.2 (35)). This analysis is in many ways (though certainly not all) consonant with the movement theory proposed in Sportiche (1987,1989). In particular, one of the ideas in these works is that core cases of extraction can only be out of complements: non-θ-marked maximal projections are absolute barriers to movement. I refer the reader to Sportiche (op. cit.) for the details of his approach.

Quite apart from adjunction, the output of the parser and the structure generated by the grammar differ in another important respect. The output of the parser reflects the absolute barrierhood of adjuncts in the strong sense that it cannot adjoin a trace to an adjunct, whereas in the grammar move α applies freely, while its effects are then subject to several constraints. We could ask (i) whether this is a problem from a conceptual point of view and (ii) whether it would be desirable to modify the grammar in such a way that its output is closer (if not identical) to that of the parser.

Before we attempt to answer these questions, let us first try to pin down *what assumptions about the nature of the grammar* make the parser's output different from the representations generated by the grammar. In chapter 3 I played down the importance of this question, focussing instead on the development of the runtime grammar with no questions asked. It is now time to make up for that omission.

To see where we are going, observe first of all that the runtime grammar makes no reference whatsoever to γ-marking. The γ-marking device is of central importance in the Barriers framework to derive the contrast between argument-operator and adjunct-operator movement out of subjects and adjuncts. In our proposal the work that is done by γ-marking in the competence theory is done by the Visibility Condition in conjunction with the assumption that Chain Composition applies in the mapping to LF. Recall that on our view the non-existence of adjunct parasitic gaps is due to a failure to construct a null-operator chain inside the adjunct that will be visible at LF. Because an adjunct-operator chain does not have a θ-marked foot, chain Composition does not apply in the mapping to LF. As the null-operator itself does not have features that delimit a range, the null-operator chain cannot escape invisibility at LF.

A second innovation is introduced by the way we have handled violations of the *Wh*-Island Condition, which on our view do not involve movement across a barrier. Instead, such violations are due to a failure to meet the very strict locality requirement imposed by our version of antecedent government.

The above assumptions involve rather drastic changes in the grammar that we started out with. Although the basic concept underlying barrierhood (viz. θ-marking) remains unchanged, we have eliminated γ-marking and the concept of inheritance of barrierhood.

Let us now return to the two questions that we set out to answer. On the sunny side of things, notice that the relation between the structure generated by the grammar and the structure generated by the parser is within the bounds of (Degenerate) Input/Output-Correspondence (cf. section 1.3.2 for an explication of this notion). Although they are not isomorphic, it is fairly obvious that we could specify an effectively computable mapping between the two. At first sight this would seem to be a nice result, because modifying the grammar to get it to generate exactly the structure computed by the parser would have the undesirable effect of introducing properties of the algorithmic level into the level of the competence theory. To be precise, the properties of the parser that give rise to the particular structure it computes are its deterministic nature and the fact that it is a machine that performs a real-time left-to-right analysis of inputs. These are properties that the competence theory deliberately abstracts away from. If there are no compelling reasons to remove these abstractions from the competence theory (the relation grammar-parser being well within the bounds of (Degenerate Input/Output Correspondence), it seems wise not to do so.

Unfortunately, matters are not as uncomplicated as one would wish them to be. This becomes apparent if we take a closer look at the *equivalence* relation that obtains between the competence grammar and the runtime grammar. The runtime grammar is certainly not metastrongly equivalent to the competence grammar: the operations of the parsing engine are not in any sense an implementation of the grammar semantics. Does the weaker relation of strong equivalence hold? Remember that for this equivalence relation to hold the competence grammar and the runtime grammar must be isomorphic (grammar compilation performs only trivial mappings). Given the above discussion, it is easy to see that they are not. Apparently, the best we can do is covering equivalence: the equivalence relation between the competence grammar and the runtime grammar that holds under (non-trivial) grammar compilation. That is, assuming that such a compilation step exists. Let me put this differently. Suppose we assume for the sake of discussion that the grammar and the parser are I/O-Correspondent. Then given covering equivalence, the competence grammar and the runtime grammar share only weak generative capacity. This would still not need to worry us, if the compilation step gave us a runtime grammar whose strong generative capacity was quite unrevealing from a theoretical point of view. But as we have seen, this is not the case. The runtime grammar embodies a number of assumptions about the nature of human linguistic knowledge that differ substantially from those of the competence grammar. For this reason this particular grammar-parser relation raises serious conceptual problems and suggests that we should try to choose between the opposed theoretical claims they embody.

Although I will not attempt to resolve the catch 22 that we have arrived at, it seems appropriate that I make a few final remarks to clarify my position. One of the discrepancies between the runtime grammar and the competence grammar lies in the assumptions about adjunction in each of these theories. We have already remarked that there is at present no theory of adjunction in the competence grammar. Failure to come up with such a theory jeopardizes the plausibility of the movement theory that one develops. This is not just true of the Barriers theory, but of any theory that suffers from the same weakness. Given this, it is entirely conceivable that assumptions that are well motivated from the point of view of parsing theory could inspire changes in the competence theory. However, as we have as yet little independent motivation for our assumptions about the nature of the human sentence processor, our judgement of the modifications of the competence grammar based on results from parsing theory should be based on the usual empirical and theory internal criteria.

Bibliography

Abney, S. (1986). "Functional Elements and Licensing". Talk held at the 1986 GLOW Colloquium in Gerona, Spain.

Abney, S. (1988). "On the Notions *GB Parser* and *Psychological Reality*". Ms. Bellcore (also appeared in *MIT Parsing Volume 1988*).

Baart J. and S. Raaijmakers (1988). "Dutch as a Deterministic Language". In P. Coopmans and A. Hulk, eds., *Linguistics in the Netherlands 1988*. Dordrecht: Foris.

Barton, G., R. Berwick and E. Ristad (1987). *Computational Complexity and Natural Language*. Cambridge, MA: MIT Press.

Bayer, J. (1984). "Towards an Explanation of Certain that-t Phenomena: the COMP-node in Bavarian". In W. de Geest and Y. Putseys, eds., *Sentential Complementation*. Dordrecht: Foris.

Bennis, H. and L. Haegeman (1984). "On the Status of Agreement, COMP and INFL in Flemish Dialects". In de Geest W. and Y. Putseys eds., *Sentential Complementation*. Dordrecht: Foris.

Berwick, R. (1982). *Locality Principles and the Acquisition of Syntactic Knowledge*. Doctoral dissertation, MIT.

Berwick, R. (1985). *The Acquisition of Syntactic Knowledge*. Cambridge, MA: MIT Press.

Berwick, R. (1987). "Principle-Based Parsing". Technical Report 972, MIT Artificial Intelligence Laboratory.

Berwick, R. and A. Weinberg (1984). *The Grammatical Basis of Linguistic Performance*. Cambridge, MA: MIT Press.

Berwick R. and A. Weinberg (1985a). "Deterministic Parsing: A Modern View". NELS 18, pp.15-33.

Berwick, R. and A. Weinberg (1985b). "Deterministic Parsing and Linguistic Explanation". *Language and Cognitive Processes* 1.2., pp.109-134.

Bever, T., J. Carroll and L. Miller eds. (1984). *Talking Minds: The Study of Language in Cognitive Science*. Cambridge, MA: MIT Press.

Bresnan, J. (1978). "A Realistic Transformational Grammar". In M. Halle, J. Bresnan and G. Miller, eds., *Linguistic Theory and Psychological Reality*. Cambridge, MA: MIT Press.

Bresnan, J. (1982). *The Mental Representation of Grammatical Relations*. Cambridge: MIT Press.

Chomsky, N. (1957). *Syntactic Structures*. The Hague: Mouton.

Chomsky, N. (1959). "On Certain Formal Properties of Grammars". *Information and Control* 2.

Chomsky, N. (1963). "Formal Properties of Grammars". In. Luce, R., R. Bush and E Galanter, eds., *Handbook of Mathematical Psychology*, Vol. II, pp.323-418. New York: Wiley.

Chomsky, N. (1965). *Aspects of the Theory of Syntax*. Cambridge, MA: MIT Press.

Chomsky, N. (1972). *Studies on Semantics in Generative Grammar*. The Hague: Mouton.

Chomsky, N. (1973). "Conditions on Transformations". In S. Anderson and P. Kiparsky, eds., *A Festschrift for Morris Halle*. New York: Holt, Rinehart and Winston.

Chomsky, N. (1977). "On Wh-Movement". In A. Akmajian, P. Culicover and T. Wasow, eds., *Formal Syntax*. New York: Academic Press.

Chomsky, N. (1980). "On Binding". *Linguistic Inquiry* 11.1., pp.1-46.

Chomsky, N. (1981). *Lectures on Government and Binding*. Dordrecht: Foris.

Chomsky, N. (1982). *Some Concepts and Consequences of the Theory of Government and Binding*. Cambridge, MA: MIT Press.

Chomsky, N. (1986a). *Barriers*. Cambridge, MA: MIT Press.

Chomsky, N. (1986b). *Knowledge of Language*. New York: Praeger.

Chomsky, N. and H. Lasnik (1977). "Filters and Control". *Linguistic Inquiry* 8.3.

Chomsky, N. (1988). "Some Notes on Economy of Derivation and Representation". In Laka, I. and A. Mahajan, eds., *MIT Working Papers in Linguistics* 10, pp.43-74.

Chung, S. and J. McCloskey (1983). "On the Interpretation of Certain Islands Facts in GPSG". *Linguistic Inquiry* 14, pp.704-713.

Cinque, G. (1984a). "A'-Bound Pro vs. Variable". Ms. Università di Venezia.

Cinque, G. (1984b). "A'-Bound Pro vs. Variable". *GLOW Newsletter* 12, pp.21-23.

Coopmans, P. (1988). "On Extraction from Adjuncts in VP". In H. Borer, ed., *Proceedings of WCCFL* 7, pp. 53-65.

Culicover, P. and W. Wilkins (1984). *Locality in Linguistic Theory*. Orlando: Academic Press.

Earley, J. (1970). "An Efficient Context-free Parsing Algorithm". *Communications of the Association for Computing Machinery* 14, pp.453-460.

Engdahl, E. (1984). "Parasitic Gaps, Resumptive Pronouns, and Subject Extractions". Ms., University of Wisconsin, Madison.

Fodor, J. (1978). "Parsing Strategies and Constraints on Transformations" *Linguistic Inquiry* 9, pp.427-473.

Fodor, J. (1985). "Deterministic Parsing and Subjacency". *Language and Cognitive Processes* 1, pp.3-42.

Fodor, J., T. Bever and M. Garrett (1974). *The Psychology of Language: an Introduction to Psycholinguistics and Generative Grammar*. New York: McGraw Hill.

Frazier, L. and K. Rayner (1982). "Making and Correcting Errors during Sentence Comprehension: Eye Movements and the Analysis of Structurally Ambiguous Sentences". *Cognitive Psychology* 14.

Gazdar, G. (1979). "English as a Context-free Language". Unpublished report, University of Sussex.

Gazdar, G. (1981). "Unbounded Dependencies and Coordinate Structure". *Linguistic Inquiry* 12, pp.155-184.

Goeman, T. (1980). "COMP-Agreement?". In W. Zonneveld and F. Weerman, eds., *Linguistics in the Netherlands 1977-1979*. Dordrecht: Foris.

Gough, D. (1965). "The Verification of Sentences". *The Journal of Verbal Learning and Verbal Behaviour* 5, pp.107-111.

Haegeman, L. (1983). "*Die* en *Dat* in Westflemish Relative Clauses". In H. Bennis and W.V.S. Lessen-Kloeke, eds., *Linguistics in the Netherlands 1982*. Dordrecht: Foris.

Hindle, D. (1983). "Deterministic Parsing of Syntactic Non-fluencies". *21st Annual Meeting of the Association for Computational Linguistics* (Cambridge, Mass.), Proceedings, pp.123-128.

Hoekstra, J. and L. Marácz (1989). "Some Implications of I-to-C Movement in Frisian". In H. Bennis and A. van Kemenade, eds., *Linguistics in the Netherlands 1989*. Dordrecht: Foris.

Hofstadter, D.R. (1985). *Metamagical Themas: Questing for the essence of Mind and Pattern*. Harmondsworth, Middlesex: Penguin Books.

Hopcroft, J. and J. Ullman (1979). *Introduction to Automata Theory, Languages, and Computation*. Reading, MA: Addison Wesley.

Hudson, R. (1984). "Multiple (Alias 'Parasitic') Gaps". Ms., University College London.

Jackendoff, R. (1987). *Consciousness and the Computational Mind*. Cambridge, MA: MIT Press.

Johnson, M. (1989). "Parsing as Deduction: the Use of Knowledge of Language". *The Journal of Psycholinguistic Research* 18.1.

Kayne, R. (1984). *Connectedness and Binary Branching*. Dordrecht: Foris.

Kaplan, R. and J. Bresnan (1982). "Lexical Functional Grammar: A Formal System for Grammatical Representation. In J. Bresnan, ed., *The Mental Representation of Grammatical Relations*. Cambridge, MA: MIT Press.

Kashket, M. (1987). *A Government-Binding Based Parser for Warlpiri, a Free-Word Order Language*. Technical Report, MIT Artificial Intelligence Laboratory.

Kashket, M. (1988). "A Principle-Based Parser for English and Warlpiri". Ph.D. proposal. MIT Artificial Intelligence Laboratory.

Koopman, H. and D. Sportiche (1982). "Variables and the Bijection Principle". *The Linguistic Review* 2, pp.139-160.

Koopman, H. and D. Sportiche (1985). "Thetatheory and Extraction". GLOW Newsletter 14.

Koot, J. van de (1985). Review of R. Berwick and A. Weinberg, *The Grammatical Basis of Linguistic Performance. Second Language Research* 1.1., pp.73-82.

Koot, J. van de (1987). "On Explaining Subjacency". In F. Beukema and P. Coopmans, eds., *Linguistics in the Netherlands 1987*, pp.121-129. Dordrecht: Foris.

Koot, J. van de (1989). "The Vacuous Movement Hypothesis, Superiority and the ECP". In G. de Haan and W. Zonneveld, eds., *Formal Parameters of Generative Grammar IV*. Yearbook 1988.

Koster, J. (1982). "Karel, Darwin en Chomsky (Over Taal en Evolutie)". In *Hollands Maandblad* 415-416, pp.3-21.

Koster, J. (1987). *Domains and Dynasties*. Dordrecht: Foris.

Knuth, D. (1965). "On the Translation of Languages from Left to Right". *Information and Control* 8, pp.607-639.

Krauwer S. and L. des Tombe (1980). "The Finite State Transducer as a Theory of Language". *Utrecht Working Papers in Linguistics* 9, pp.1-86.

Kuroda, S.-Y. (1986). "Whether We Agree or Not: Rough Ideas about the Comparative Syntax of English and Japanese". Ms. University of California at San Diego.

Lasnik, H. (1985). "Illicit NP Movement: Locality Conditions on Chains?". *Linguistic Inquiry* 16, pp.481-490.

Lasnik, H. and M. Saito (1984). "On the Nature of Proper Government". *Linguistic Inquiry* 15, pp.235-289.

Lerdahl, F. and R. Jackendoff (1983). *A Generative Theory of Tonal Music*. Cambridge, MA: MIT Press.

Lightfoot, D. and A. Weinberg (1988). "Review Article on *Barriers*".*Language* 64, pp. 366-383.

Longobardi, G. (1988). *Symmetry Principles in Syntax*. Unipress: Padua.

Marcus, M. (1980). *A Theory of Syntactic Recognition for Natural Language*. Cambridge, MA: MIT Press.

Marcus, M. (1987). "Deterministic Parsing and Description Theory". In *Linguistic Theory and Computer Applications*, P. Whitelock, M. Wood, H. Somers, R. Johnson and P. Bennett, eds., London: Academic Press.

Marcus, M., D. Hindle and M. Fleck (1983). "D-Theory: Talking about Talking about Trees". *Proceedings of the 21st Annual Meeting of the Association for Computational Linguistics* (Cambridge, Mass.), pp.129-136.

Marr, D. (1982). *Vision*. San Francisco, CA: Freeman.

May, R. (1985). *Logical Form*. Cambridge, MA: MIT Press.

McMahon, L. (1963). *Grammatical Analysis as Part of Understanding a Sentence*. PhD dissertation, Harvard University.

Miller, G. (1951). *Language and Communication*. New York: McGraw-Hill.

Miller, G. and N. Chomsky (1963). "Finitary Models of Language Users". In R. Luce, R. Bush and E. Galanter, eds., *Handbook of Mathematical Psychology* vol. 2. New York: John Wiley.

Neijt, A. (1979). *Gapping*. Dordrecht: Foris.

Nijenhuis, W. (1989). "Vergelijking van de Marcus Parser met een LR(k) parser". MA thesis, University of Utrecht.

Nozohoor-Farshi, R. (1986). "On Formalizations of Marcus's Parser". COLING 86, *Proceedings of the 11th International Conference on Computational Linguistics*, pp.533-535. University of Bonn. August 1986.

Pesetsky, D. (1981). "Complementizer-Trace Phenomena and the Nominative Island Condition". *The Linguistic Review* 1, pp.297-343.

Rizzi, L. (1987). "Relativized Minimality". Ms. Université de Geneve/Stanford.

Rizzi, L. (1988). "On the Status of Referential Indices". Ms. Université de Genève.

Rosenberg, A. (1967). "Real-time definable languages". *Journal of the Association for Computing Machinary* 14, pp.645-662.

Ross, J. (1968). *Constraints on Variables in Syntax*. PhD dissertation, MIT. Reproduced by the Indiana University Linguistics Club.

Savin, H. and E. Perchonock (1965). "Grammatical Structure and the Immediate Recall of English Sentences". *Journal of Verbal Learning and Verbal Behaviour* 4, pp.348-353.

Slobin, D. (1966). "Grammatical Transformations and Sentence Comprehension in Childhood and Adulthood". *Journal of Verbal Learning and Verbal Behaviour* 5, pp. 219-227.

Sportiche, D. (1987). "Unifying Movement Theory". Ms., USC/UCLA.

Sportiche, D. (1989). "Syntactic Movement: Constraints and Parameters". Talk held at the 1989 GLOW Colloquium in Utrecht, The Netherlands.

Stowell, T. (1981). *Origins of Phrase Structure*. PhD dissertation, MIT.

Taraldsen, T. (1981). "The Theoretical Interpretation of a Class of 'Marked' Extractions". In A. Belletti, L. Brandi and L. Rizzi, eds., *Theory of Markedness in Generative Grammar*. Pisa: Scuola Normale Superiore.

Walker, E. et al. (1968). "Grammatical Relations and the Search of Sentences in Immediate Memory". *Proceedings of the Midwestern Psychological Association.*

Weerman, F. (1986). "The Different Faces of Verb Second". Ms. University of Utrecht.

Wehrli, E. (1984). "A Government-Binding Parser for French". University of Geneva, Institute for the Study of Semantics and Cognition Working Papers, no. 48.

Weinberg, A. (1988). *Locality Principles in Syntax and in Parsing*. PhD dissertation, MIT.

Weinberg, A., J. Aoun, N. Hornstein and D. Lightfoot (1987). "Two Types of Locality". *Linguistic Inquiry* 18.4.

Williams, E. (1984). "Grammatical Relations". *Linguistic Inquiry* 15, pp.639-673.

Index

A'-antecedent 109
A-antecedent 109
Abney, S.P. xii, 5, 16, 18-24, 36, 133, 141
Activate, primitive parser action 47
Active and inactive grammar rules in Marcus parser 125
Active node stack 43, 51-54, 90, 92
  accessibility of 46, 74, 92, 95, 98, 99
  and encoding of left context 70
Adjacency 28, 74, 80
Adjunct Condition 4, 88, 93, 108, 120, 121, 132, 135, 137
Adjunction
  and grammar size 107
  to VP 83-85, 93
Algorithmic theory 8, 20, 27, 35, 37, 97, 133, 138
Ambiguity
  local 40, 50, 55, 61, 73, 111
Annotation of active node 75, 76, 95, 99, 100, 102
Antecedent government
  definition 105
  redefinition 114
Artificial Intelligence 11-13, 30, 32, 37, 55, 97, 141, 143
Aspects of the Theory of Syntax 6, 20, 135, 142
Assertion sets (see also minimal commitment parser) 55, 59
Attach, primitive parser action 47
Attachment
  immediate 90-93, 96, 109
Attention shift in Marcus parser 49
Attention Shifting rules 49
Automata
  finite 19, 20, 43, 70, 72
  pushdown 43, 44
Automaton
  Characteristic Finite State Machine 72
  finite state 43
  pushdown 43
  shift-reduce 44
Autonomy of syntax 30, 31, 55
Baart, J. 141
Backtracking 40, 61, 121
Barrier 81-86, 88-90, 93, 114, 115, 122, 124, 130, 138
  definition 83
  redefinition 114
Barton, G.E. 26, 29, 107, 141
Bennis, H. 128, 141, 143
Berwick, R. 1-3, 5, 22, 26-30, 33, 39, 46, 54-58, 64, 67, 68, 70, 72-78, 80, 91, 96, 107, 113, 118-120, 134, 135, 141, 143, 148, 149
Bijection Principle 117, 119, 121, 123, 124, 143
  definition 123
Birnbaum, L. 31
Blocking category 81, 82
  definition 82
Bottom-up parser 44, 45, 49, 69
Bounded Context Parser 39, 68, 96, 134
  and left context 72
  formal properties of 69
Boundedness
  characterization of 3, 80, 81
Bounding Condition 74
Bounding node 78
Bresnan, J. 26, 27, 141, 143
Buffer
  in Marcus parser 3, 17, 39, 42, 43, 45, 48, 50, 54-56, 59, 61, 62, 64-66, 69, 70, 73, 96, 134
  virtual 49
C-command 27, 83, 116, 121, 124, 129, 137
  definition 83
CED (Condition on Extraction Domains) 88, 89, 99
Centre-embedding 19-21, 24, 35, 37
Chain

composition 115-117, 121, 136, 138
formation 4, 98, 100-103, 108, 113, 129
Chain Composition 115-117, 121, 136, 138
Chain Condition 122
Chain Optimization 123
Characteristic finite state machine 72
Chomsky, N. xi, 1, 3, 5-7, 11, 14, 15, 16, 19, 24, 25, 27, 30, 31, 32, 39, 56, 67, 69, 77, 80, 81, 83, 84, 86, 88, 89, 90-93, 96, 101, 102, 105, 109, 115-117, 122, 127, 129, 131, 134, 136, 137, 141-144, 148, 149
Chung, S. 80, 134, 142
Cinque, G. 142
Coindexing 68, 86, 101
Competence theory 4, 8, 10-14, 16, 26, 27, 28, 31, 35, 37, 97, 135, 138, 139, 140
Competence-performance distinction 1, 2, 5-7, 10-14, 24, 28, 30, 31, 35, 50, 141, 143, 147, 148
Complementizer agreement 128
Complex NP Constraint 78, 80, 89, 94
definition 78
Condition on Chain Links (CCL) 104, 106, 125, 131
Context-free grammar 16-19, 23, 28, 29, 43, 79, 107, 142
Correspondence
metastrong 22, 24
strong 21
weak 19, 20, 24
Create, primitive parser action 47
Current domain
definition 92
Current node 1-3, 15, 32, 43-48, 53, 54, 66, 70, 73-76, 80, 90, 92-95, 99, 103, 106, 109-112, 114, 116, 121, 125, 126, 133, 137
Cyclic node 46, 75
Data driven 42, 45
Data structure 40
Deactivate, primitive parser action 47, 48, 51, 52
Derivation
rightmost 69, 71
Derivational Theory of Complexity (see also DTC) 1, 2, 5, 24, 25, 134, 147
and the Standard Theory 25, 28, 32
Des Tombe, L. iv, xi, 22, 144
Description theory (see also minimal commitment parser) 55, 144
Determinism
and functional explanation 3, 5, 9, 26, 33-36, 39, 56, 73, 74, 75-78, 80, 96, 120, 131, 132, 134, 141, 143
and Marcus parser 2, 3, 39, 40, 41, 45, 91, 93
strict 2, 41, 45
Determinism hypothesis 2, 3, 39, 40, 41, 45, 91, 93
Diagnostic rule 42, 49
Domain
definition 92
Drop, primitive parser action 47, 67, 90, 93, 95, 110
DTC 39
failure of 25, 30, 32
Earley algorithm 16, 29
Earley, J. 16, 18, 19, 22, 28, 29, 142
Empty Category Principle (ECP) 86, 87-90, 95, 101, 102, 118, 127, 131, 143
definition 87
Equivalence
covering 22, 32, 68, 139
D-I/O 21-24, 33-35, 37
I/O 16, 18, 19, 21-24, 33-35, 37, 139
metastrong 22-27
strong 21-23, 26, 139

Exclusion
  definition 83
Finite control
  in Marcus parser 67, 70, 73, 74, 79
  use of essential variable in 74
Fodor, J.D. 2, 25, 33-36, 64, 68, 74, 75, 131, 134, 142
Frazier, L. 2, 61, 62, 64, 142
Functional account 34-36, 75, 120, 131, 132, 134
  type 1 34, 35, 131, 132, 134
  type 1 and the Natural Computation Framework 35
  type 2 34-36, 134
  type 3 34, 36, 131, 132, 134
Functional description 56
Functional explanation 3, 5, 34, 39, 73, 74, 75, 77, 78, 80, 96, 120, 131, 134
  of subjacency 3, 39, 73-75, 80, 134
Gamma-checking 87
Gamma-marking 3, 4, 86-89, 91, 92, 98, 112, 114, 137, 138
  definition 86
Garden path sentences 20, 27, 33, 41, 42, 50, 55, 59, 62-65
Garrett, M. 25, 142
Gazdar, G. 28-30, 107, 142
Generalized Phrase Structure Grammar 3, 28-30, 78-80, 96, 107, 134, 142, 149
Generalized Phrase-Structure Grammar
  and complex nonterminals 78, 79
  and parsing efficiency 28
Generative capacity
  strong 139
  weak 139
Generative grammar 6, 24, 142, 143, 145
Gough, P. 25, 143
Government
  definition 83
Grammar
  (psychological) reality of 2, 14, 16, 133, 141
  runtime 3, 4, 18, 29, 31-33, 35, 40, 50, 68, 97, 98, 109, 110, 131, 138, 139
  Standard Theory 25, 28, 32
  transformational 1-3, 6, 7, 11, 13, 23-28, 30, 32, 33, 39, 73, 141
Grammar rule interpreter 16, 18, 19, 40, 46, 49
Grammar-parser pair i, iii, 1-3, 5, 16, 19, 21, 23, 26, 27, 31, 33, 35, 76, 98, 133-135, 139
Haegeman, L. 128, 141, 143
Hardware level 10, 11, 15, 20, 21, 36, 37
Hindle, D. 143, 144
Hoekstra, J. 128, 143
Hofstadter, D. 13, 143
Hopcroft, J. 143
Hypothesis driven 42
I-language 15
Information-processing problem 12, 13, 37, 97
Insert, parsing action 47, 48, 51, 69, 74, 76, 93, 126
Insert, primitive parser action 48
Intractability 107, 131
Jackendoff, R, xi, 63, 143, 144
Johnson, M. xi, 2, 143, 144
Kashket, M. xi, xii, 10, 143
Kayne, R. 92, 143
Kintsch, W. 30, 31
Knuth, D. 71, 144
Koopman, H. 100, 123, 143
Koot, J. van de iii, 39, 74, 80, 143, 151
Koster, J. 36, 143, 144
Krauwer, S. xi, 22, 144
Kuroda, S. 100, 103, 144
L-marking 81-83, 85, 86, 90, 91, 93, 96
  definition 82
Label, primitive parser action (see also annotation) 47
Language faculty 14, 37
Lasnik, H. 39, 86, 101, 102, 142,

144
Left context
accessibility of 46, 74, 92, 95, 98, 99
Left-to-right constraint 46
Level of description
algorithmic level 8, 20, 27, 35, 37, 97, 133, 138
competence level 8, 10, 11
hardware level 10, 11, 15, 20, 21, 36, 37
Lexical rule
as replacement for transformation 26, 30
Lexical-functional grammar 26, 143
Lexicon, entries in 26, 49, 62, 98, 113, 116, 117
Longobardi, P. 129, 144
Lookahead 39, 50, 59, 96
and local ambiguity 61
and wait-and-see strategy 55
apparent counterexamples to 54, 59
in Bounded Context Parser 69
in LR(k) parser 69-72, 96, 134, 144
in LRRL(k) parser 69-72, 96, 134, 144
LR table 19
LR(k,t) parser 71
LR(k) parser 68-70, 75, 96, 134
formal properties of 69
LR(k) table 70
LRRL(k) parser 1, 69, 72, 75, 77-80, 96, 97-99, 102, 108, 113, 134, 135
and encoding of left context 75
and feature annotation 75
and subjacency 78
formal properties of 69
LRRL(k) table 79
Machine
recognition of spoken language 9
vision 9
Marcus parser 2, 3, 19, 32, 39, 40, 41, 43, 45-47, 50, 54, 59, 64, 66, 67, 69, 70, 72, 74, 75, 91, 92, 96, 97, 109, 110, 113, 131, 132, 134, 148, 149
and determinism 1, 4, 26, 39, 40, 42, 54-56, 61, 67, 70, 72, 73, 75, 81, 95, 96, 98, 108, 113, 116, 121, 131, 134, 135, 137, 139, 141, 142, 143, 144
and lookahead 3, 17, 39, 42, 43, 45, 48, 50, 54-56, 59, 61, 62, 64-66, 69, 70, 73, 96, 134
and parsing analogue of Projection Principle 69, 73, 91, 92
and top-down prediction 43, 70, 71-75, 78, 80, 95
and use of active node stack 43, 51-54, 90, 92
as LRRL(k) parser 1, 69, 72, 73, 74, 75, 77-80, 96-99, 102, 108, 113, 116, 134, 135
formal properties of 69
relation to Bounded Context Parser 39, 68, 96, 134
Marcus, M. xii, 1-3, 19, 32, 33, 39, 40-43, 45-47, 49-55, 59-61, 64, 66, 67-70, 72-76, 90-92, 96, 97, 108, 109, 110, 113, 131, 132, 134, 144, 147-149
Marr, D. vi, 2, 5, 7, 8, 10-14, 20, 21, 32, 37, 68, 144, 148
McCloskey, J. 80, 134, 142
McMahon, L. 25, 144
Mechanism
implementation 10-13, 33, 34, 39, 41, 43, 46, 49, 66, 70, 72, 86, 96
Metarules
computational complexity of 29, 107
Metasemantics 23, 24
Miller, G. 5, 19, 24, 30, 59, 109, 141, 144
Minimal commitment parser 54, 55, 60, 61, 64, 96
Minimality Condition 77, 90, 125,

144
Move α 137
Necker cube 20
Neijt, A. 75, 144
No-counting argument 77, 80, 135
Normal rules 48
Nozohoor-Farshi, R. 69-72, 96, 134, 144
NP-movement 75, 77, 99-101, 108
One-one mapping 18, 19, 21, 32
Operator
  adjunct 86, 87, 89, 104, 117, 138
  argument 86, 87, 138
  null 114-121, 123, 124, 129-132, 136, 137
Packet control in the Marcus parser 46, 48, 49, 51-54, 67, 76, 110, 114, 121
Parasitic gaps 4, 99, 114-117, 119-124, 129, 131, 132, 136-138, 142, 143
  and chain composition 115-117, 121, 136, 138
Parser
  bottom-up 42
  Bounded Context 68
  Bounded Context Parser 39
  data driven 42
  deterministic 40
  LR(k,t) 71
  LR(k) 68, 69
  LRRL(k) 69, 72, 75, 78
  Marcus parser 39
  modified Marcus parser 67
  shift-reduce 44
  top-down 42
  two-stage 68
Parsing 54
  and encoding of left context 70
  and successive cyclic movement 70
  LR(k) 68-73, 75, 96, 134
  LRRL(k) 1, 69, 72-75, 77-80, 96-99, 102, 108, 113, 116, 134, 135
  minimal commitment 54, 55, 60, 61, 64, 96
  of adjuncts 59, 108
  with assertion sets 55
Parsing complexity
  and grammar size 29
  as evidence against theory of grammar 28
  of Marcus parser 68
Parsing engine 18, 19, 23, 24, 33, 36, 40, 116, 139
Passive 4, 26, 100, 104, 110, 131, 135
  super-passive and deterministic chain formation 4, 100, 104, 131, 135
Pattern-action rule format 46
Perchonock, E. 25, 145
Pop, primitive parsing action 17, 44, 47, 53, 111, 112
Predicates
  linguistic 121
  non-counting 74, 76, 78, 80, 96, 97, 108, 135
Priority of grammar rules 46-48, 53, 54
Processing
  bottom-up 44, 45, 49, 69
  left-to-right 46, 55, 72, 117, 139
  parallel 3, 7, 40, 61, 63, 121, 128, 132
  serial 25
  top-down 42, 44, 45
Proper government
  definition 86
Psychological reality 2, 14, 16, 133, 141
Quasi-arguments 117
Raaijmakers, S. 141
Raising 4, 87, 100, 104, 131, 135
  super-raising and deterministic chain formation 4, 100, 104, 131, 135
Rayner, K. 2, 61, 62, 64, 142
Reductionism 71, 72
Referentiality 68, 116, 117, 119, 144

Rightmost derivation in reverse 69
Ristad, E. xii, 26, 29, 107, 141
Rizzi, L. 77, 117, 127, 128, 144, 145
Rosenberg, A. 29, 144
Ross, J. 78, 144
Rules
as mental computations 6
pattern-action 46
Runtime grammar 3, 4, 18, 29, 31-33, 35, 40, 50, 68, 97, 98, 109, 110, 131, 138, 139
Saito, M. 86, 144
Savin, H. 25, 145
Schank, R. 31
Semantic biasing 55, 64, 67
Shift-reduce parser 44
Size of grammars and parsing complexity 29
Slobin, D. 25, 27, 145
SPEC-head agreement 83, 85, 93, 94, 126-128
Sportiche, D. 4, 100, 104, 123, 137, 143, 145
Stack Accessibility 92
Standard Theory 25, 28, 32
State
accept 43-45, 54
initial 14, 17, 43, 44
State set 17, 18
Stowell, T. 145
Subjacency 3, 39, 73-78, 80, 81, 86, 88, 89, 93, 95, 96, 102, 115, 120-122, 131, 134, 136, 142, 143
bounding nodes for 28, 74, 80
definition 74
Functional explanation of 73, 75
Subject Condition 4, 88, 94, 108, 132, 135
Taraldsen, T. 145
Theta-government
definition 86
Theta-marking 112
Token-token identity 21
Top-down strategy 44
Trace creation 95, 106, 108, 124
Transformation
as mental operation 6
as precomputed grammar rule 26
inverse 5, 25-27, 30, 32, 39, 147, 149
Transformational grammar
and the DTC 5, 25-27, 30, 32, 39, 147, 149
realization by Marcus parser 32, 33, 39, 41, 42, 59, 60, 65, 67, 68, 76
Ullman, J. 143
Unbounded left context 74, 75, 95
Universal Clausal Skeleton (UCS) 114, 122
Vergnaud 118
Virtual buffer 49
Visibility Condition 116, 118, 119, 123, 137, 138
definition 116
definition in Berwick & Weinberg (1985a) 119
Vision
line detection 9
machine 9
Walker, E. 25, 145
Weak generative capacity 139
Weerman, F. xi, 142, 145
Wehrli, E. 2, 145
Weinberg, A. xi, 1, 3, 5, 22, 27, 28, 30, 33, 39, 46, 54-62, 64, 67, 68, 72, 73, 74-78, 80, 84, 91, 96, 107, 118, 119, 120, 134, 135, 141, 143-145, 148, 149
Wh-Island Condition 3, 77, 80, 96, 102, 131, 134, 135, 138
Wh-movement 56, 75, 82, 87, 88, 99, 103, 108, 110, 124, 142
Williams, E. 26, 145
X-bar theory 26, 56, 69, 81, 100
and position of D-structure subject 100, 103, 144

Bei Fragen zur Produktsicherheit wenden Sie sich bitte an:
If you have any questions regarding product safety,
please contact:

Walter de Gruyter GmbH
Genthiner Straße 13
10785 Berlin
productsafety@degruyterbrill.com